INDIVIDUALIZING EDUCATION THROUGH CONTRACT LEARNING

INDIVIDUALIZING EDUCATION THROUGH
EDUCATION
THROUGH

CONTRACT LEARNING

NEAL R. BERTE

General Editor

The University of Alabama Press

University, Alabama

CONTENTS

Preface   vii

Contributors   xi

PART ONE   ISSUES

1   Individualizing Education Through Contracting   3
NEAL R. BERTE

2   Goal Development and Assessment of   12
Educational Resources
BERNARD J. SLOAN

3   Evaluation of Individualized Learning   21
HAROLD L. HODGKINSON

PART TWO   CASES

4   Learning Contracts at New College, Sarasota   33
JAMES FEENEY AND GRESHAM RILEY

5   Developing Intellectual Competence at Empire State   62
ARTHUR CHICKERING

6   Contracting in a University Without Walls Program   77
ARGENTINE S. CRAIG

7   Bringing About Change in a Traditional   97
Institution by Learning Contracts
NEAL R. BERTE

8   Out-of-Class Learning and Contract Learning   122
    at Justin Morrill
    JOHN DULEY

9   Beyond Contract Curricula to Improvisional Learning   144
    JOHN BILORUSKY AND HARRY BUTLER

10 The Future for Learning Contracts   173
    NEAL R. BERTE

    Bibliography   187

    Index   191

PREFACE

The concept of individualizing education for students through contract learning is one which has gained increased prominence in higher education in recent years. Probably most educators would agree that the individualization of learning is a good ideal, but they would admit that it is extremely difficult to accomplish. Can it be done economically? Who should decide the goals for the educational experience—the student, or others who may have more knowledge and experience on which to base their decisions? Who should be involved in judging the achievement of these goals—only the professor, or other faculty members? How should this achievement be evaluated? And can the integrity of the college or university be preserved when individualized learning is encouraged outside the traditional campus environment?

This volume is an attempt to consider both the philosophical bases and these practical realities of individualization through the analysis of various approaches to the contract learning process. The first three chapters serve as an introduction to contracting. Chapter One develops the concept of contract learning and attempts to set it in perspective within the larger context of higher education. Chapter Two discusses the goal development process in contract learning—a critical ingredient in this approach to college education. And Chapter Three examines the evaluation of individualized programs with an emphasis on the diagnostic, flexible, and learner-centered approaches to assessment that can be employed in contract learning programs.

Part Two offers illustrations of the diversity involved in the contract learning movement. Chapter Four presents a critical analysis of the use of contract learning by the pioneer institution which first adopted this approach in 1964—New College at Sarasota, Florida—and juxtaposes freedom and authority as the context for this approach. Chapter Five demonstrates the use of learning contracts for the new adult clientele of Empire State College in New York. Chapter Six also deals with adult students but within a University Without Walls setting: that at Morgan State University in Maryland. Chapter Seven demonstrates the use of contract learning in bringing about change in a traditional institution through a case study of New College at The University of Alabama. Chapter Eight analyzes the out-of-class learning options available through contractual arrangements at Justin Morrill College of Michigan State University. Chapter Nine takes a more theoretical approach in utilizing the concept of contract learning for "improvisational learning" particularly in the human service professions. The final chapter draws heavily on these previous case studies in providing a taxonomy of contract learning programs as well as a discussion of strengths and problems of this approach to college education.

The institutions represented in this volume were chosen because of the diversity of approaches they represent in using the contract learning concept and also because of the quality of the leadership provided at these institutions by the authors of the several chapters. These cases aim to provide the particular and practical information needed by educators who are contemplating the use of learning contracts in their own institutions. I am grateful to the authors of these individual chapters for their contribution. Others involved in the preparation of the book who deserve appreciation are Elaine Hughey Barnes and Edward O'Neil, two graduates of the New College at The University of Alabama, who provided research assistance. I am particularly grateful to Harold Hodgkinson for his work as consulting editor for the project and to J. B. Hefferlin for his support and assistance.

It will be obvious to the reader of this book that contract learning means different things to different people in terms of changed roles for faculty and students, implications for the educational mission of institutions, techniques for teaching and learning, and fiscal realities of higher education. It will be equally obvious that the use of contract learning will not be a panacea for the ills of higher education. But as American colleges and universities open up a greater variety of educational paths and create a more diverse series of options to meet the needs of their students so that each of them can maximize their opportunities in higher education based on their own aims and interests, contracting offers a useful approach to this end. I hope this book enables more institutions to use this approach.

University, Alabama   NEAL R. BERTE
November 1975

TO
ANNE, BECKY, JULIE,
MARK, AND SCOTT

CONTRIBUTORS

Neal R. Berte is vice-president for educational development of The University of Alabama and dean of its New College.

John Bilorusky is the assistant director of the University Without Walls Program, Berkeley, California.

Harry Butler is chairman of the department of social services at Cleveland State Uinversity.

Arthur Chickering is vice-president for policy analysis and evaluation at Empire State College.

Argentine S. Craig directs the University Without Walls program at Morgan State College described in this article as well as the Urban Regional Learning Center for the Union for Experimenting Colleges and Universities.

John Duley is assistant professor and director of the Field Study Program of Justin Morrill College at Michigan State University.

James Feeney is assistant dean at the Long Island Regional learning Center, Empire State College, State University of New York in Old Westbury.

Harold L. Hodgkinson is project director at the Center for Research and Development in Higher Education, University of California, Berkeley.

Gresham Riley is provost of New College, where he has taught philosophy since 1965.

Bernard J. Sloan is associate dean of the New College at The University of Alabama, project director for its External Degree Program, and coordinator of Out-of-Class Learning.

INDIVIDUALIZING
EDUCATION THROUGH
CONTRACT LEARNING

PART ONE

ISSUES

1 NEAL R. BERTE

Individualizing Education Through Contracting

Over the past decade, the terms *contract* and *contracting* have developed at least three new uses in American higher education: growth contracting, contracting for grades, and learning contracts. All three concepts are related, but each is distinct; only the third is the major subject of this volume.

Growth contracting involves a faculty or staff member agreeing with an administrative superior or colleague at the beginning of a contract term, such as the academic year, about his responsibilities and obligations during this period, emphasizing particular areas of professional growth. At the end of the term, the two discuss progress over the period, thus encouraging self-evaluation and reflection by the faculty or staff member about his aims, interests and accomplishments.

Contracting for grades involves an agreement between a teacher and a student at the beginning of a course as to the grade the student expects to receive and the amount and quality of work he is expected to produce to earn this grade. In this way, students are aware of what is expected of them right from the start of the course and they can progress without the fear and anxiety associated with ambiguous expectations or evaluations (Dash, 1970).

Learning contracts, though not binding documents in the strictly legal sense of *contract,* are written agreements or commitments reached between a student and a faculty member or committee regarding a particular amount of student work or learning on the one hand and the amount of institutional reward or credit for this work on the other. They can cover various lengths of time, any

3

amount of work, and all disciplines or areas of knowledge; but they typically contain at least four elements: (1) a statement of the student's goals for the particular learning experience, (2) the methods by which the student aims to accomplish these goals, (3) the evaluation measures to be employed in assessing this achievement, and (4) the amount of credit to be awarded the student as a result of the achievement.

The concepts underlying learning contracts—that the arrangements for learning can be mutually negotiated between a student and a teacher, and that this mutual agreement in advance is desirable in the learning process—are among the newer ideas in the historic process of adapting schools and colleges to the individual needs of their students. By extending the individualization of instruction to new dimensions, learning contracts provide an answer to endemic problems of every educational instiution: regimentation, irrelevance, and student passivity.

LEARNING CONTRACTS IN THE LARGER CONTEXT OF HIGHER EDUCATION

The concept of individualizing educational experiences and of a more central role for students in the teaching-learning process has characterized all recent major commission studies, including those by the Newman Task force, the Carnegie Commission on Higher Education, and the Commission on Non-Traditional Study. All argue for more variety in college programs, for more alternatives in curricula, and for a greater emphasis on meeting the needs of individual students rather than for pre-packaging educational experiences with the assumption that those experiences are right for all. Their recommendations are epitomized by the statement from the Commission on Non-Traditional Study which serves as a continuing theme for this book: "We are talking about an attitude that puts the student first and the institution second, concentrates more on the former's need than the latter's convenience, encourages diversity of individual opportunity, and de-emphasizes time and space or even course requirements in favor of competence and, where applicable, performance" (1973, p. 5).

We know that students entering college today differ widely in their abilities, their high school experiences, their goals, and their demographic backgrounds. It seems inevitable that the demand will become even greater in the future for a wider spectrum of educational activity from which such students may choose. These demands certainly will not sweep aside traditional education in American colleges and universities, as there is much of enduring value now being taught. But more and more colleges and universities will be expected to create more diverse options for their students, and learning contracts will afford both institutions and students one major approach to these options.

The history of American higher education is replete with examples of prior approaches to individualizing the undergraduate experience. Most famous, of course, is the elective system—ranging from President Eliot's "free elective" plan at Harvard to the more common plans of allowing students to select courses from among a variety within several broad areas such as the humanities or the sciences. Others have included multiple tracking and ability grouping; joint majors, interdisciplinary majors, and student-designed majors; alternate paths to meeting specific degree or competency requirements; independent study; directed readings; and individual tutorials. All these efforts have contrasted with the nineteenth century Lancastrian system of mass producing students through a totally prescribed and regimented sequential curriculum.

The basic behavioral principle from which all of these efforts at individualization have stemmed is that of individual differences —the fact that students differ so greatly in their personal characteristics, such as their readiness for learning, their motivation for learning, and the amount of their past learning, that institutions will be more effective if they fit their educational programs as much as possible to their students' individual needs. The psychological evidence supporting this principle has been accumulating for the past hundred and fifty years. Recent developments in American higher education have made its implementation more urgent than before.

First, the philosophical basis of American higher education has continued to become more egalitarian in terms of opportunities for more students to attend institutions of higher learning. As a result, the student community is now highly diverse in ability, age, academic and occupational interest, past achievement, and goals for the educational experience.

Second, our concept of which groups are included in the learning society has been broadened by a new definition of postsecondary education which recognizes not only those in the 18-to-21 age range enrolled in colleges and universities, but also learners of any age in proprietary institutions, business and industry, labor unions, prisons, home, and volunteer educational programs. In this regard, the entry of more adult students and the return of other older students to higher education has major implications for individualization of instruction, as the idea gains acceptance that schools and colleges are responsible not only for educating the young but also for reeducating the middle aged and elderly.

Third, the knowledge explosion compounds the question of what an educated person should know. Because of this uncertainty, the task of higher education becomes less the imparting of specific knowledge and more the development of skills and techniques for continued self-education.

Fourth, the growth of external degree programs in this country has provided a great impetus to the recognition of new learning modes and to the ideas that what one knows may be more important than how that knowledge was gained. The increased acceptance by many institutions of credit by examination and credit for past learning experiences—witnessed by the fact that over one thousand institutions now grant credit for successful performance on the College Level Examination Program—is likely to increase expectations that institutions will meet the student where he is rather than prescribe educational experiences in a restricted way.

Fifth, the feeling of anonymity and helplessness on the part of many students brought about both by the large size of today's campuses and by the heavy reliance on computers and other mechanized processes for registration, record keeping, and in some cases even advising deserves attention by colleges and universities if they are concerned with treating students as human beings and individuals.

Sixth, today's students in the 18-to-21 age range—still the majority of those enrolled in higher education, despite increased enrollments from older adults—are more mature, both physiologically and socially, by about a year than those a decade ago; they have greater knowledge by the time they enter college, largely because of the pervasive news media; they are freer from want because of today's affluence; they are more mobile geographically and socially; and by the time they get to college, many of them are "grouped out." They have been members of Cub scouts, Brownies, youth groups, and various organizations throughout elementary and secondary school; and may be more free to express their individuality during college than previous generations.

Seventh and finally, educational leaders and scholars are calling on higher education for realignments to meet these and other pressures. Dixon, for example, warns of the dissonance created when students find the curriculum "too rigid and ill adapted to their individual interests" (1967, p. 13); Ericson, discussing *The Individual and the System,* advocates a two-way interchange between the on-campus curriculum and the world off campus and the replacement of teacher-centered instruction with an emphasis on individual student learning needs (1967, p. 85); and Baldwin warns that "the lock-step pattern of attendance and the traditional degree requirements prescribe so thoroughly the goals that individual students are to pursue that the student is left passive in the face of the institution" (1973, p. 55). As a result, more and more educational institutions are making their resources available to students so that they can tailor-make programs to meet their own needs rather than be shuttled through pre-packaged sets of requirements. Although in most institutions there still may be a considerable amount of prescription and "shuttling," the availability of various options and choice points is significantly affecting the educational experience of many students.

THE UNIQUE CONTRIBUTION OF LEARNING CONTRACTS

Among the several means by which colleges can individualize their programs, contracting offers certain unique features. It not only requires student initiative—typical of most others— but also student responsibility for goal setting and goal achievement and student skill at persuasion and negotiation. Unlike most indepen-

dent study projects, it requires students to specify at the beginning
their intentions and plans in a formal way so that their achievement
can be assessed with reference to their original commitment. In
short, it combines freedom and responsibility in a structured form:
if a student wants the freedom to choose what he desires to study,
he must also accept the responsibility of active pursuit. As Dressel
points out, the contractual procedure is a valuable learning process
in itself, apart from the substantive material to be learned: it
"helps the student to set his own goals and to be responsible for
their realization" (1971, p. 61).

The fact that people learn what they want to learn and what
they commit themselves to learn—and therefore the need for student involvement in the selection of learning experiences—represents an idea propounded not only by contemporary educators
but by philosophers of earlier centuries. Thus to Socrates and
Plato, teachers were mere midwives who might help a youth give
birth to his soul. In providing such assistance, they taught nothing
but instead stimulated the youth's analytic ability and perceptive-
ness. One may recall those lines from *The Republic,* "bodily exercise, when compulsory, does no harm on the body; but knowledge
which is acquired under compulsion obtains no hold on the mind."
In contrast to much contemporary regimented educational practice,
the pedagogy of these teachers was based on the conviction that
from the beginning the student was inalienably free and ultimately
responsible.

The quadrivium and the trivium of the Middle Ages went far
in conceiving knowledge to be a fairly fixed body of information
permitting little room for student centered experiences; and the
impersonal and highly structured curriculum which has characterized most institutions of higher learning until recently has not permitted students a very significant role in shaping their curricular
experiences. Even when the principle of individual differences has
been recognized, it has all too often been used in adjusting different students to a common program rather than in creating the
options for students to maximize their own interests and desires.

With the decline of *in loco parentis* in the extracurriculum, the
burden for curricular decisions has also shifted from the faculty to
the individual student. Yet students often face the multiplicity of

options and decisions with less support from faculty, let alone parents and other adults, and even from their peers, than in the past. Learning contracts allow faculty to play the role of intellectual midwife and advisor, rather than that of parent. Under this approach, faculty members no longer assume the role of telling students what they should take. Instead, their responsibility is diagnostic—that is, to assist the student with the development and clarification of learning goals, self understanding, and self direction—and evaluative, in terms of assessing the student's achievement on agreed-upon measures: not prescriptive and punitive.

Bronfenbrenner indicates that in many relationships between children and adults, "to the extent that the child gets any attention at all in response to his own activity, it is likely to be when he misbehaves to the point of interfering with the adult." The same dynamic too frequently exists at the college and university level, where professors may indicate to their classes that they are available by appointment during office hours for students who have "problems" related to the course. Similarly, the student personnel staff of most colleges and universities goes to great lengths in making themselves available to students with problems. The implication, of course, is: "If you don't have a problem, don't take up my time." Contract learning programs, however, necessitate the involvement of faculty who are concerned with the development of students as individuals and who are willing to work with students as advisors—not only just in cognitive development but also in social and emotional growth.

Contract plans, as their name implies, necessitate the agreement of at least two parties. Contracts are mutually negotiated between a student and a faculty or staff member or a faculty committee; and most plans expect students and their advisors or mentors to discuss the proposed contract in person before formalizing it in writing. This negotiating relationship with an adult frequently marks a student's initial growth from childhood status to increasingly independent status.

Moreover, the first component of the learning contract usually is the specification of general and immediate goals as the foundation for the student's educational experiences. When one contemplates the number of students who slide through college without ever articulating their goals, it is interesting to see the contract model as forcing students to consider such questions as "Who am I?" "Where do I want to go?" "How do I want to get there?" Some students who have entered a contract program after spending a few years in more traditional curricula in other colleges report that it is the first time any faculty member has asked them these basic questions—and, often, that it is the first time they have pursued them themselves. While it is recognized that it is difficult for many students to assume an active role in clarifying their own learning goals and purposes, and thus while contract learning may *not* be desirable for those students preferring a prescribed set of learning experiences, the clarification of personal goals is an integral part of learning contracts.

In short, learning contracts attempt to provide individualized flexibility to students, as do other approaches to individualization, while at the same time emphasizing student initiative, involvement, and responsibility in educational decisions, together with advisory support from faculty and other staff members within the academic community, and a more adult relationship between students and faculty in considering students' goals and planning their programs.

GROWTH OF THE LEARNING CONTRACT APPROACH

Based on the most recent information available, it is estimated that over three hundred colleges and universities are using learning contracts either for their total programs or as optional features either for courses or for special types of learning such as out-of-class and off-campus experiences. These institutions do not, by and large, restrict contracts to any particular length of time or any particular disciplines; but there appear to be several operational models for the contract in terms of content: One emphasizes primary concern for vocational or professional competence as the overriding goal of the contract. Others emphasize an academic approach either to a discipline or interdisciplinary work, while still others take a problem-oriented approach or involve an aesthetic learning experience for the student.

Colleges and universities are taking varied routes to the creation of contract learning programs. Some have transformed their total curriculum; others have substituted contract learning as an alternative to various courses; and still others have made only minor modifications such as adding the option to existing courses of allowing students to contract for grades. Because of the diversity in approach taken by different institutions in terms of their distinctive educational missions and their differing clientele, the case studies which follow in succeeding chapters deliberately include a wide variety of contracting plans. They range from total institutions employing contracts, such as Empire State College and New College, to special units and cluster colleges of traditional institutions, such as Morgan State, Michigan State, and the University of Alabama. All of them, however, exemplify the concept of students contracting for *learning,* and not merely for grades in traditional courses. They illustrate the practical consequences of contract plans, such as enrollments, financial requirements, and changed faculty roles; and they indicate the potential that learning contracts have for further individualization of higher education and for a greater role for students in shaping their own education.

2 BERNARD J. SLOAN

Goal Development and Assessment of Educational Resources

Learning is one of the most personal of all human endeavors. The basic assumption of contract programs in education, therefore, is to facilitate the idea that each individual's educational goals are the primary consideration for significant learning. The importance of goal development in contract learning programs can be seen on both the individual and the institutional levels. Although we are concerned principally with the individual, a prerequisite for good programs is having the appropriate milieu for individual goal development, and any plans for student goal development should, therefore, begin with the goals of the institution wherein the contract program is to be based.

How can one begin to develop institutional goals for a contract program? John Dewey, an important figure all too often overlooked when considering current developments in non-traditional education, postulated that " . . . the central problem of an education based upon experience is to select kinds of present experiences that live fruitfully and creatively in subsequent experiences." (Dewey, 1938). Dewey called this the principle of *continuity*, because it emphasizes the idea of looking to the future in experiential programs. Coterminous with this principle is the principle of *interaction*, which recognizes the fact that cognitive and affective forces are present in any learning situation and should be recognized and incorporated into the fundamental precepts of any strategy seeking to foster experiential learning. Dewey thought that "continuity and interaction in their active union with each other provide the measure of the educative significance and value of an experience." (Dewey, 1938) Here we have two criteria by which to develop institutional goals. Benjamin Bloom, in *Taxonomy of Educational Objectives; Handbook I; Cognitive Domain,* posits four basic questions which elucidate some basic principles in institutional goal formulation. These are: "1) What educational purposes or objectives should the school or course seek to attain? 2) What learning experiences can be provided that are likely to bring about the attainment of these purposes? 3) How can these learning experiences be effectively organized to help provide continuity and sequence for the learner and to help him in integrating what might otherwise appear as isolated learning experiences? 4) How can the effectiveness of learning experiences be evaluated by the use of tests and other systematic evidence-gathering procedures?" (Bloom, 1956).

In developing institutional goals, then, the following should be considered: the programs should be designed for working with students on an individual basis. They should not have a procrustean nature; they should embrace the concept of education as a continuing process; they should be forward-looking in development and in evaluation so that students can build future programs out of the needs and experiences derived from previous ones; they should seek to enhance affective as well as cognitive forces; they should provide for appropriate skill development; and institutional goals should be designed to embrace summative evaluation (evaluation that attempts to assess an experience in its entirety—usually accomplished at the end of an experience) as well as formative evaluation (evaluation which seeks to assess an on-going experience in order to have in-progress impact on the experience).

Another institutional responsibility in a contract learning program is the provision of an appropriate system of student advising. A statement that appears frequently in the literature concerning contract programs is the plea for better advising, yet this remains an area of great need. There are several advising models including the tutor or mentor relationship which implies an academically oriented advising function. There is the full-time academic counselor model, in which the advisor is often seen by students as functioning in an administrative role, usually involved with test giving, schedule arranging, and credit negotiations. Often this type of counselor is forced into an adversary role with students. Another kind of advisor is the peer counselor. While peer counselors may be more accessible and more concerned about the affective issues that surround the learning process, they are frequently selected without careful attention to interpersonal skills and knowledge of complex academic problems and are given little training to help alleviate their deficiencies.

Current responses to the need for new advising models deserve consideration. One example is the concept of the Learning Consultant which is being developed by the Learning Consultant Network of the Regional Learning Service (RLS) of central New York. This program is based on the assumption that programs for non-traditional learners will not be effective without facilitating systems which are themselves non-traditional. RLS uses members of the community in the advising process, and the advisors come from offices, community organizations, schools, and professional associations. These advisors are selected initially because they are persons with whom external degree candidates in the Regional Learning Service would come in contact in the normal course of their learning experiences. RLS staff members select those who already possess many of the personal skills important to the advising relationship and give these people "in-service" training to further enhance their skills. The Learning Consultant Network is thus able to incorporate a variety of styles into an advising role that is flexible enough and functional enough to meet the diverse needs of those involved in external degree programs. (Vickers, 1973).

Another interesting advising program of a non-traditional nature is the program at Johnston College, University of Redlands. The advising program there is centered around "laboratories in personal and social growth." Here the students and faculty are involved in various types of sensitivity training or T-grouping where individual uniqueness can be revealed and where a student can get a deeper understanding of himself. These sensitivity sessions are combined with class and community activities involving the faculty of Johnston College, always with an emphasis on personal growth.

The continuing ability to be self starting is a desirable outgrowth of 'coping' skills learned in this training. Through exposure to the attitudes basic to the laboratory method (emphasis on the individual's readiness to relate to the real world, to life, in the present moment), Johnston College seeks to establish a practical bridge between academic tradition and the 'outside' world. (Elmendorf, 1971).

Each year there is an opening all-college community laboratory which provides a setting for the entire community to plan together, evaluate, and relate to basic college goals, while at the same time this occasion provides an opportunity for concentrated personal growth experiences for all working with professional facilitators.

A third example of non-traditional advising is the development of student-to-student counseling programs at several institutions. Most noteworthy perhaps is the program at Southwest Texas State University under the direction of William F. Brown. (Brown, 1965) In this program students are given extensive and systematic training in preparation for their advising and then they play a prominent role in the advising process—often with pay.

Now let us consider some very specific elements that are necessary to facilitate goal development as a function of advising. For our purposes goals can be understood as expectations that exist at varying levels of awareness with the student. It is the role of the adviser to help the student to articulate these expectations and to organize for their pursuit. Much of the following may seem elementary, but the fact remains that very few advising programs place goal development and advising in an individualized context.

First there must be an advisor who understands the concept of individual differences and who perceives advising students as a major professional responsibility. This presumes, of course, certain institutional attitudes toward the faculty reward system, since advising should be seen as a fairly important function and rewarded accordingly. Next, the student should be made aware of the available advising services, encouraged to use them, and offered adequate and specific opportunities for this advising to take place. Students should also be made aware of the available resources such as student services, placement and testing, along with the opportunities for out-of-class learning. An advisor who takes his responsibilities seriously is of primary importance.

Matching advisors with students is another important matter. Certainly the student should have choices, but often this is not possible—for example, with new students who do not know appropriate advisors for their situations. One approach is to assign a primary advisor to all new students with the understanding that as goals become clearer and as the student's awareness of the resources available to him increases, the student will select his own advisor or team of advisors.

In the initial stages the advisor should lead the student to an understanding of several concepts. First of all the student should understand that the principal responsibility for his development rests largely with the student and not with the institution. This will not always be an easy task because most students will not know how to cope with such a revolutionary concept. Next the student must be led to perceive a need for goal development. This may be accomplished by something as simple as inquiring about the goals of the individual student. The student may not have thought about his future in terms of goal development, and the question "What are your educational goals?" may not be thoroughly understood at first. This leads to asking "What is goal development?"—a useful question because few students understand this concept. Goal development is a process of continuous change with *goal setting* being only one part of the process. Every learning activity has impact on goal development by confirming a goal already set or by providing data that lead to goal alteration. Too many advising programs skip from episode to episode of *goal setting* and provide little framework or little encouragement for students to perceive the changing nature of the *goal development* process or the opportunity to capitalize on self-understanding inherent in this process.

The typical advising program often sees a student meeting a faculty member once or twice a year, perhaps even less, and if the question of goals is discussed at all it usually involves trying to identify a set goal and gives little attention to the larger and continuing process of goal development. In leading a student to develop his or her own goals, the advisor should encourage the student to examine the information available, to seek new information concerning goals, and to consider the vocational implications of the available choices. If a radical departure from a previous goal is involved, students should be encouraged to assess the risk and cost involved in the alternatives that seem to be available, as well as to understand the goal development process which has taken place. Then they should be helped to outline strategies for pursuing the new goals. A major part of the advising process should be raising the consciousness of students about the fact that goal altering is an expected activity because change and growth is basic to the human condition. The student should understand that he or she should not feel undue anxiety if a lifelong or childhood goal should suddenly change upon exposure to new information.

With this concept of continuous change in mind the student should be led to recognize that the process of change based on his experiences—both academic and non academic—should be understood in terms of the future. The question should be asked at every point, "Where does this previous development lead us?" The idea of continuous change mandates continuous feedback. Hodgkinson maintains that assessment procedures and their results should be available continuously or certainly as often as a student thinks he needs feedback. The motivational aspects of goal development should be as much as possible intrinsic rather than extrinsic, which prevents the feedback from having to be labelled in an evaluative way except in terms of the student's past performance since this is the only reference group which is truly significant (Hodgkinson, 1971a). Continuing feedback must be facilitated by the ready accessibility of the advisor on an informal basis along with designated or scheduled meetings with the student. One meeting per academic term is barely a satisfactory minimum. Also there should be as much collaboration as possible, with the student playing an important role in goal development. This tends to negate the possibility of any adversary or "generation gap" relationship developing. (Hodgkinson, 1971a). Since advising should emphasize improvement of the student's strength as well as efforts to minimize weaknesses, a lowered threat level between the advisor and student should emerge. They should become collaborators working for the student's best interests.

One of the important aspects of goal development is providing the appropriate setting for goal development to take place. This setting should help to encourage students to develop their own identity and their own system of values. This can be done by putting them into situations that will bring them into contact with value systems different from those they have known in the past so that their own ideas can mature. An out-of-class learning experience for academic credit is one excellent device for increasing self-understanding as well as for testing vocational goals. Students should be made aware of all resources available for experiential learning both on and off campus. The development of resources is a vital activity to which we will turn later in the chapter.

The following assumptions should characterize an advising process based on concerns for individual goal development: (1) there must be competent advisors present in order to facilitate goal development; (2) the advisors must understand the principle of individual differences; (3) the responsibility for goal development rests largely with the student and not with the institution; (4) there must be adequate contact between the advisor and the students playing a major role in the collaboration; (5) goal development is a continuing process and merits continuing feedback; (6) available resources must be made known to students; (7) the advising process should attempt to improve on students' strengths as well as their weaknesses; and (8) there must be an appropriate milieu beyond the advising sessions in which goal development may occur.

An individualized advising process which places heavy emphasis on goal development provides several advantages. It offers the students an opportunity to participate actively in the design and implementation of his learning process, and it provides maximum flexibility for recognizing the importance of individual differences among students in planning their educational programs. Since the student is heavily involved in the advising process, the experiences planned in each advising session are more likely to be those for which he is ready and which are challenging to that individual. This procedure maximizes the possibility of developing an educational program which relates learning to previously developed interests of the student and may likely win him to the intellectual enterprise. This procedure also provides opportunities to develop close personal relationships with faculty members who know the student well and who are willing to assist the student in identifying personal capacities and limitations. (Ottawa University, 1970). We have discussed the importance of making students aware of the available learning resources as a function of goal development. Many learning resources will be identified and maintained within the context of the institution, e. g., formal classes, labs, practica, and independent study options; yet many other resources may be discovered and developed in out-of-class experiences. In fact the student, if given the opportunity, may add greatly to an inventory of learning resources, especially those resources that are available beyond the classroom. There is much value in having a student locate and organize many of his own learning opportunities since this supports the important concept of shifting responsibility for learning from the institution to the student even in this important area of developing resources. Traditionally, of course, assessment of learning resources has been an institutional process with students playing at best a minimal role. The institutional self study for accreditation, rather than development of a learning resources inventory for use in advising students, is often the motive for such assessment. Thus it may be necessary for advisors in a contract learning program which emphasizes individual goal development to work with the students in developing files on learning resources both on and off campus.

To select among various options, advisors and students should consider several questions before deciding on a particular learning experience, whether in a classroom or not. First, "How does the resource relate to the student's educational goals, and is it consistent with institutional goals?" This question is especially important if a large amount of student time is to be invested in the particular resource. It is also important to determine whether the resource leads to other learning experiences and provides for both cognitive and affective learning (i. e., whether the experience satisfies the principles of continuity and interaction). Advisor and student should discuss what linkages a particular learning resource can provide with previous scholarship and decide how best the total experience can be evaluated—in terms of cognitive and affective growth, skill development, acquisition of theoretical knowledge and so forth. Both formative and summative evaluation strategies should be planned and included in the contract before the student embarks on a learning experience. The experience will provide the learner with opportunities to examine, exercise, and expand his or her own system of values, thus furthering the overall process of goal development.

To sum up briefly, there are some basic principles common to student goal development and the assessment of educational resources in contract learning programs. First, learning is a personal activity and is best achieved in an institutional setting when the institution fosters learning as a function of individual goal development. Second, the responsibility for learning should rest primarily with the student and not with the institution. Third, evaluation procedures should be an early consideration in any learning experience, and they should, so far as possible, be designed to assist the learner in developing subsequent educational goals; that is, they should be future, rather than past, oriented. The principles of continuity and interaction should be a guide in seeking and assessing learning experiences. Fourth, goal development is an open-ended, continuing process—merely goal setting is not enough. Fifth, traditional models of advising are often not the best for facilitating goal development and new models should be sought for these purposes. Sixth, the contract model is an excellent organizational device to facilitate the implementation of these principles. It is axiomatic in any decision making process that the clearer one's goals the easier decisions become, and contract programs, along with their concomitant advising procedures, maximize this principle of individual goal development.

3 HAROLD L. HODGKINSON

Evaluation of Individualized Learning

When one thinks about college level evaluation, one typically thinks of a procedure whereby we rank one student's score on some standardized measure against the other students whose scores form the form for that measure. Although norm-referenced procedures can still be used in evaluating individualized programs, it is quite clear that they are often inappropriate and that their domination of the process has been reduced. As one individualizes learning, one necessarily individualizes the processes of evaluation, and it is at this point that the situation begins to get complicated. The more we individualize learning, the more the student needs diagnostic information to perform mid-course correction maneuvers which will make it possible for him to improve on a continuous basis, using feedback from the evaluative process as he goes. Thus, evaluation becomes partially a way of *improving,* not just measuring learning. In addition, we will want to know whether or not the student attains the goals that were decided; but, as Carol Weiss has said, the acquisition of preconceived goals is only one measure of performance and leaves out other unintended components of student learning which may be equally useful. Individaulized learning means working individual student differences into the learning process rather than ignoring them. Evaluation, in order to be consistent, should be flexible, at least partially diagnostic, and centered on the goals of the individual learner. As the learner improves, more of the evaluation process should be in his or her hands through *self*-evaluation.

This problem of evaluation of individualized learning is getting increasingly important, due mainly to the trend in many, if not most, institutions to consider granting credit for prior life experiences as well as present off-campus experiences such as field experience and foreign study. Many campuses have resorted to a cut-off score on an instrument such as CLEP, but when one looks at the arbitrary fashion in which these institutional cut-off points are established, the process seems less than equitable. The crediting of all out-of-class learning should be based as much as possible on the circumstances of the individual learner. A variety of evaluative devices will allow the development of a triangulation of where the student actually is, using a variety of standardized tests, self-anchoring scales, simulations, reports from supervisors, logs, diaries, teachers' reports, use of prior learning in new settings, etc. Such a triangulation procedure, although sometimes more costly, should result in more accurate credit-giving than through any one instrument.

An additional force leading to a focus on evaluation comes from the new interest in accountability and consumerism in higher education—is the student actually getting what he or she paid for? States are asking the cost-effective questions of institutions—what is the yield, or return, on a dollar of scarce state capital invested in higher education compared to other services designed to improve the quality of life? The first attempts at outcome measurements (credit hours generated per FTE faculty, degrees awarded per FTE faculty, etc.) were at best only proxy measures of student learning. Increased interest is now being shown in developing some measures of educational "value added"—how far has each individual student moved from his or her point of entry?

Before pursuing the question further, it might be helpful here to say a word about what is meant by individualized programs. I do not consider that a student working by himself or herself is necessarily engaged in an individualized program if what the student is doing has been entirely pre-determined by someone else. The essence of individualized programs is that the student participates in the formation of the learning activity; it is to some degree self-initiated and self-directed. For example, a language lab is not necessarily an individualized program of instruction, and neither is the audio-tutorial as the notion is commonly used. These devices are active response producers and that is usually better than having the student in a passive mode, but I do not believe that active responses to another's directions are enough. Were that the case, seminars would produce significantly higher levels of student learning than do large lecture classes, and unfortunately this has never been demonstrated. What does matter about individualized programs, it seems to me, is that it must be the *learner's decision* to enter into and partially to structure the activity. Although the evidence is not yet in, I tend to support the view that what will produce greater gains in measured student acquisition and retention of knowledge will be self-initiated work.

The same problem applies to the term "independent study." A student studying all by himself is not necessarily engaged in independent study. The decision as to what and when study takes place must be made by the student with advice and consultation before the program can be truly said to be independent. This means that a student who voluntarily decides to take Introduction to Biology as a large survey course and is allowed by the instructor to structure the course to meet his or her needs via the Keller Plan, may be engaged in an independent activity which could qualify as independent study. Another student who is sitting by himself reading through the teacher's outline and reading list for a particular course is simply taking that course on a one-student basis. I dwell on this point because we usually think that the term "individualized program" is easily understood in that most of us agree on what it is—a single student working alone. I would argue that one on one is not enough—you can have an individualized learning program with 10 or 15 students in a group all doing pretty much the same thing and in a collaborative way, as long as each student has the right of decision. The focus needs to be on the *decision to want to learn, what to learn, and how to learn it.*

I would argue that research has taught us very little about the decision to want to learn. (It is also interesting that we know almost nothing about how people forget.) We can, however, find out some very interesting things about the processes which make people want to learn, and this, it seems to me, is at the heart of individualized instruction. It does not mean complete carte blanche to the student, as he or she should be asked to defend choices to a skilled and competent mentor or advisor. The decision should basically be the student's, which is then ratified or reviewed by the faculty.

One major problem in the evaluation of *all* types of learning is that the measuring device is usually tacked onto the end of the learning sequence, as the final exam is in most courses. This seems not so useful as the building of evaluation strategies into the learning process itself, making them available when they are needed to check student progress and to diagnose learning difficulties in order to maximize the student's level of mastery. Indeed, in many forms, the evaluation process can become one of the most important learning outcomes for the student as he or she moves toward greater *self*-understanding through a well designed evaluation strategy. This is certainly the case in contract learning, in good modularization, in field experience programs, and in many competency-based curricula. This view, that evaluation (for the improvement of student learning) is a continuous, integral part of the teaching and learning strategy, is a marked contrast to the traditional view that only the final, or summative, evaluation is of any importance. Even if a student does well on a final exam, the norm-referenced "A" is of no use in helping the student improve. (Some students say that getting an unexplained "A" is more frustrating than getting an unexplained "C" or "D"*.) Certain endpoint evaluations are necessary for credentialing and other purposes, but they often interfere with teaching and advising functions.

For this reason, it seems to me to be increasingly important that we separate out the functions of teaching (basically communication), advising (basically diagnosis), and credentialing (basically norm-referenced evaluation to see if a person meets some external, often job-related, norm). Many individualized learning programs may not have any credentialing components as such. And many individualized learning programs can proceed without a great deal of formal teaching.

One of the most useful procedures for the evaluation of individualized programs is the learning contract. In this form, the student and his advisor agree in advance on the nature of the learning to be done, the way in which this learning fits into the student's

* H. Hodgkinson, "Bard Students Correct Themes on Tape."

larger objectives, and how it can be determined whether or not the student has actually fulfilled his goals. Both the faculty member and student sign it, and the learning contract becomes the evaluation base. Learning contracts do separate teaching, advising, and credentialing functions. Indeed, if the contract is well drawn, the evaluation and diagnostic processes should be continuous, as well as final. The contract should have within it formative and summative dimensions.

The evaluation component here, as in all other cases, should endeavor both to improve performance and to ascertain whether stated goals have been achieved. In many cases, individualized learning programs have a point of view or ideology which runs into direct conflict with the notion of a grade system. Yet it may well be that grades can be useful if agreement on the meaning of the grade is decided upon in advance with the individual student.

It should be pointed out that a number of instruments are available which will give both an aggregate and individual score on a number of dimensions of personal functioning. Instruments like the Omnibus Personality Inventory, the Allport-Vernon, the Institutional Functioning Inventory, the Experience of College Questionnaire, and the Pace-HEMEK can be used both to develop norms on groups of students and as a pre-post test measure of individual student change through time. It is sad but true that at this writing none of these instruments has been developed to indicate the normal, or expected, changes in student scores through the freshman-senior time period. Only Astin's work with the ACE data bank can yield expected scores on the measured variables for seniors based on scores of entering freshmen at that institution. However, if faculty have been trained to use it properly, an instrument like the OPI can be of great diagnostic use in programs of individualized instruction. However, without adequate training, introduction of testing results into the advisory and diagnosing arena can be a disaster for the student. (Hodgkinson, 1974.)

In many field experience programs, some very good self-rating scales have been developed, providing highly individualized responses as well as a common framework for their interpretation. Many of the University Year for Action programs are also producing very rigorous yet individualized evaluation instruments for actually measuring the amount of student change stimulated by the field experience. As one example of what might be learned in this area, Edward Angus from Mars Hill College, long a leader in field experience education, has reported that students decline markedly on measures of authoritarianism after the field experience. Before they go out, they are fairly sure that there are only two kinds of people, good and bad, etc. After the field experience, which puts many of these students into a brand-new environment for the first time, they have begun to integrate into their own world view the complexities and ambiguities that comprised the field situation, moving from Perry's stage of absolute certainty to relativistic concerns. In these circumstances, the personality measure was useful in documenting the impact of a field experience program on a particular kind of student body.

I personally do not like the idea of having students choose between learning contract models of different levels of difficulty— an "A" contract for those who wish to work hard, a "B" contract for those who don't wish to work quite so hard, etc. It seems to me that a contract should be a unique and indigenous thing and should not be subject to comparative judgments. However, for certain kinds of individualized programs, grades may be useful. It should be pointed out here that, as Peter Elbow has said in the *Journal of Higher Education,* what grades really measure is the affective quality of the teacher's response to student learning. "A"'s and "F"'s are significant in that they indicate genuine pleasure or genuine pain as the instructor's perception of the student's work. "B"'s and "D"'s indicate the same thing to a lesser degree, while a "C" means that the instructor had no affective response to the student's performance at all.

It seems to me much better, both in learning contracts and in competency-based learning programs generally, to develop criteria in a checklist form which can be gotten to the student early enough to be useful. It can be used a number of times, and if the student wishes he can use it as a "time line" chart, something like those used in hospitals to chart patients' progress. It can be multi-dimensional time-line indicating 5 or 6 areas of the student's growth as they relate to the contract or other individualized form of learning agreement. The most important thing is the elimination of the domination of a one-dimensional model of evaluation for individualized programs. Within a class, it may be possible to develop a common checklist for outcomes, if the ways of attaining those outcomes are unique or at least well distributed among members of the class. Thus, one can have common goals attained through individualized means. Again, the major criterion is whether or not the student is personally committed to learning a specific thing in a specific way.

Any criterion for evaluating student progress, like grades, checklists, etc., should begin to wither away as the student spends more time in the institution, leaving the senior with well developed abilities to accurately assess his or her own performance without these external aids. Indeed, there should be a major difference between the freshman and the senior, in that the senior should have developed effective ways of analyzing performance effectiveness and ways of knowing when goals have actually been attained. There may be some aggregate measures of this that are extremely useful. (One that has occurred to me on a recent trip to Eckerd College in Florida was a visit to the school bookstore and a conversation with the manager. The manager revealed that freshmen are very heavy on monogrammed beer mugs, sweatshirts, and T-shirts, but that the seniors won't go near this kind of thing. This indicates to me quite clearly that *some* developmental pattern has taken place whereby the seniors as a group have different sets of values than the freshmen. These unobtrusive measures may be useful to institutions wishing to assess whether individualized programs are making any difference to the student body as a whole.)

It seems clear that many faculty members do not have the skills to do good diagnostic and evaluative work in helping students with individualized learning programs. Very little in the typical faculty member's experience has trained him in this area. Indeed, some graduate schools even now are still recommending that the faculty member consider the student simply as a vessel into which knowledge is to be poured. A number of faculty development centers have now been started in the United States, most of them designed to help faculty members improve their teaching. Some of these institutions are beginning to devote considerable time to the development of faculty skills in advising. Empire State, Ottawa, Eckerd, and Minnesota Metro, among others, have discovered that good "mentors" need different kinds of skills than the typical faculty member possesses.

One of the skills necessary in effective faculty participation in individualized instruction is the process of helping the student isolate the nature of the task he or she wishes to undertake. This is a diagnostic situation that may involve something like the "taking of a case history" in the medical profession. These are clearly trainable skills, and there is some evidence that many faculty have improved noticeably in this particular area of professional work. Particularly in contract learning, the faculty member is often the principal initiator of the evaluation design for that particular student's work. This makes it more imperative than ever that in contract learning faculty members develop a variety of flexible evaluation tools. The other approach (and I think it is a less effective alternative) calls for some staff member with skills in this to review all contracts to make sure that evaluation designs are feasible and legitimate.

Another problem which faculty members need assistance on concerns the fact that students' goals can, and often should, change through time. This means that the contract and the evaluation design within it should be susceptible to the addition of "mid-course correction maneuvers" whereby the evaluation design can be modified as the student moves through the program. This is not to be seen as a "lowering of standards," as the final evaluation model may be much more rigorous after the student has a more accurate picture of what it is that he or she wants to attain.

A final set of questions involves the impact of individualized learning programs on a college campus. Here we are discussing not the evaluation of an individual student's program but rather the aggregate analysis of what individualized learning programs as a whole have meant to the life of the college. What would be a reasonable expectation for a college which went heavily into a program of individualized learning, especially through contract models? Here are a few *possible* items which would suggest the impact of such programs on campus:

1. Shifts in library usage, both in terms of hours of the day and

types of materials used. (A broader spectrum of materials in circulation rather than a heavy concentration on a small number of reserve books.)

2. Different patterns of student life in the residence and dining areas.

3. Different student patterns of traffic flow on and off the campus.

4. Some shifts in faculty load calculation and faculty feelings of where their professional interests center.

5. Massive complaints from the registrar that things are getting out of hand.

6. More informal student-faculty interaction over meals in the residence halls etc.

7. Stronger feelings of student involvement with their education, expressed through questionnaire inventories, changes in personal behavior, and greater production of student-initiated work.

8. Greater criticism of the evaluation structure in conventional classroom settings as a result of the student's having developed his own evaluation design for his learning contract.

9. Some shifts in the attrition rates, and the number of students who take some time off before graduating. (One would anticipate a larger number of students taking some time off, but in addition the possibility of a larger percentage of the entering class graduating at some time in the future.)

One of the major needs that emerge for faculty in this kind of program is for the development of more sophisticated evaluation models and a broader spectrum of possible evaluation designs for faculty members who work with individualized programs. The need is great in graduate schools which increasingly will be turning out new Ph.D.'s who presumably should have these skills and yet in reality do not. In addition, in-service programs to help develop these skills in existing faculty are also very important.

One natural outgrowth of this line of thought, emphasizing increased individualization of learner outcomes, is an increased concern with the development of individualized notions of teacher competence. This means that certain teachers may wish to develop greater skills in advising or seminar teaching, while others may wish to increase their competence in module writing, working in teaching teams, etc. The next logical outgrowth is the idea of *dif-*

ferentiated staffing—different teachers can do different things in order to reach a full-time load, rather than figuring faculty load strictly on the number of courses taught. Individualized learning leads directly to notions of individualized teaching, encouraging each teacher to develop those learning-producing skills which most interest that instructor. However, differentiated staffing assumes that the institution is willing to *pay for* educationally related services, such as advising, committee service, supervising independent study, producing plays and art exhibits, and other highly individualistic skills, by including them in calculations of faculty load.

It may well be then that individualized learning programs may begin to force the issue of defining what a faculty member's professional areas of skill should be. Those areas in which he is supposed to be professionally competent he must be held accountable, and the institutions that train college teachers (or educate them) will have to be held accountable for inculcating these skills in the neophyte teacher-to-be. In the long run, the movement toward individualized instruction may be very helpful in terms of developing competent teaching faculty who see teaching pluralistically, as the total number of activities, engaged in in a variety of settings, which produce student learning. The focus should shift from good teaching to good learning, some of which requires no teaching at all.

PART TWO
CASES

4 JAMES FEENEY AND GRESHAM RILEY

Learning Contracts at New College, Sarasota

Colleges, like governments, wield both power and authority. Although closely related, power and authority are really quite different. Power is the ability or capacity to exercise control over others. Authority, on the other hand, is the capacity to control others where the others accept the control as legitimate and proper. Power can always be augmented; authority once lost is infinitely more difficult to restore. A crisis exists in higher education today because the power of colleges and universities has lost authority.

Nowhere is power's loss of authority more evident than in the area of curricula. A curriculum can be understood as a college's conception of relevant knowledge and as the learning process operationalized. Colleges, throughout most of the history of American higher education, have been able to control their students' programs of study, imposing clearly refined conceptions of knowledge. They have been able to do so with the concurrence of students who have accepted, however grudgingly, such control as legitimate and proper. In short, the power of colleges and universities to operationalize the learning process in a manner they deemed proper has been surrounded by an aura of authority.

The coalescence of power and authority with respect to curricula resulted historically from a number of factors. Among the more important ones were:

> The prestige of colleges and universities that derived from the value placed on them by the society at large.
> Society's belief that competence and "respectability" were in some way augmented by the socialization process which took place in institutions of higher learning.

The instrumental value of the Bachelor of Arts degree in securing for a student the "good life" within American society.

The respect afforded faculties by virtue of their being the agents of the socialization process and the ones responsible for generaing new knowledge.

The confident consensus among faculty members as to what a student must learn in order to be an educated man or woman. Out of this consensus emerged required courses, distribution requirements, and rigorously structured majors.

So long as the above factors defined the context within which higher education conducted its business, it was difficult to conceive of a serious challenge to the power of colleges to impose authoritatively a higher structured curriculum.

Possibly, the most important development in higher education during the late 1960s and the early 70s has been the atrophy of the traditional sources of collegiate authority such as those just cited. For example:

The prestige of colleges and universities which supports their authority suffered serious blows. On the one hand, they were seen as havens from which radicals could attack other institutions with impunity. On the other hand, the universities themselves were found to be intimately involved with conservative economic and military policies which came under widespread attack. In the face of these complaints from right and left, higher education's claim to scholarly detachment was attenuated.

Young people, liberated by increased wealth, mobility, and the relaxation of many traditional constraints on behavior, increasingly valued working with their hands and participating in the expressive arts. "Respectability," in the eyes of the young, could be attained in ways other than putting in four years at the college of their choice.

The instrumental value of many degrees, particularly those in the liberal arts and the sciences, declined due to "overproduction" of degree-holders and growing employer awareness that possession of a liberal education was not necessarily related to on-the-job competence.

The respect once afforded faculties lessened due to student skepticism as to the relevance of much of the new knowledge academicians generate, the value of the socialization process of which they are the agents, and the extent of their commitment to teaching as opposed to furthering their own careers through research, publication, and consultantships.

The cumulative effects of years of growing specialization in the academic disciplines left few scholars who could agree among themselves as to what constitutes a liberal education.

The result of this breakdown of traditional sources of authority which is a phenomenon characteristic of more than just higher education institutions, is that the authority of colleges and universities has become marginal in relation to society in general and to students in particular. Increasingly, there has emerged among students a "take it or leave it" attitude with respect to imposed curricula. Consequently, the ability of colleges to operationalize a given conception of knowledge has become problematical.

In the face of a loss of authority, a standard ploy by organized groups is to resort to intimidation, expulsion of dissenters, and even brute force. Fortunately, none of these options is really open to a college or university, no matter how readily they may be used by governments. The relationship between institutions of higher education and their "subjects" is voluntary, and the "subjects" can withdraw as they please with what seems to be increasingly minimal consequences. It is against the backdrop of the untenability of compulsion and the breakdown of traditional authority that the educational contract must be viewed. In their attempt to remain viable, colleges are seeking devices which hold the promise of restoring their waning authority. The contract system of education is one such device. In this essay we will look at a particular learning contract system and explore its effectiveness as a substitute for more traditional sources of collegiate authority.

The learning contract, when used as the central curricular strategy, is predominantly student—and faculty—centered. Reminiscent of the elective system, it offers even greater flexibility because the educational contract is not tied to a classroom, credit-hour structure. The contract represents a far more fundamental departure from tradition than its similarity to the elective system would suggest, however, for it shifts authority away from the institution toward the individual faculty member and the student. The relationship between mentor and student emerges as fundamental; the institution becomes little more than a mechanism for bringing the two together and for providing the auxiliary services required in order to make a recognized academic degree available. Whereas formerly curriculum committees, deans, and/or departments legitimized decisions and demands, maintained performance standards, and structured roles, individual faculty members working within a contract system find that they and the students are the final arbiters.

The contract system of education is enmeshed, therefore, in an apparent paradox, and it is best that this paradox be recognized clearly at the outset. As we have already suggested, the contract is, on the one hand, an interesting development due to its potential for restoring *institutional* authority in the area of the curriculum. On the other hand, the manner in which a contract system actually functions is such as to shift curricular authority from institutions to *individuals*. What appears on the surface, therefore, as a promising corrective to waning collegiate authority may in operation only compound a difficult situation. We will return to this issue in the concluding section of the essay.

The contract system of education presented here is that of New College, Sarasota, Florida, a coeducational liberal arts college granting the Bachelor of Arts degree. Opened in 1964 as a private institution, New College became New College of the University of South Florida 1 July 1976 as the result of a unique merger between the college and the State University System of Florida. As an honors college of the University, New College will remain on its Sarasota campus and will be financed by a combination of public and private funds. It will retain its distinctive educational program, with the learning contract system as the organizing principle of the curriculum.

In 1971 the present contract curriculum was adopted. Its adoption was a response, in part, to the significant decline in graduate school applications by New College students after 1968. In addition, the contract system was a response to an increasing student demand for participation in the design of their programs of study and an acknowledgment of the difficulty which a faculty has in constructing any curriculum resting on shared intellectual and pedagogical assumptions.

The central requirement of the new curricular structure was that for each of three ten-week terms in an academic year a student must formulate a contract with a single faculty sponsor. Working with the sponsor, the student was expected to articulate in the contract both short- and long-term educational as well as career goals; the specific academic and experiential activities by means of which the goals would be pursued; and finally, the evaluative criteria in terms of which the contract would be certified as fulfilled. Final certification of student performance was to be made by the sponsor on a pass - no credit basis, and the contract itself rather than credit hours or course units was to be the basic ingredient in the undergraduate degree. Nine satisfactorily completed contracts (up to four of which could be pursued in off-campus, field experience projects); four satisfactorily completed independent study projects; and a senior research project successfully defended in an oral "baccalaureate examination" constituted the requirements for the B.A. Theoretically, the options for contract design and content were to be completely open, for there were no distribution, language, or other "general education" requirements in the curriculum. A detailed explanation of New College's learning contract system follows, excerpted from a document presently used by the College to acquaint new students with the program:

THE NEW COLLEGE EDUCATIONAL CONTRACT

INTRODUCTION

At New College we believe that the primary aim of education is to nourish individual growth. To accomplish this our educational environment has a rich array of people and opportunities which can be related to you through a unique curricular device we call the Educational Contract. Your responsibility is to find out about our resources and use the curriculum to facilitate exploitation of them.

Every aspect of the college, from the contract and the non-graded curriculum to the unmonitored dormitories, assumes you will take responsibility for your self. *You* must reach out into the college community and tap its resources. The traditional "props" of grades, required class attendance, dormitory parietals, and the like are gone. People are here to suggest possibilities and challenge you to new levels of understanding and creativity, but they cannot insure that you will become involved in your own development. Only you can do that. The importance of your own inner motivation will become evident as you confront the challenges in creating a contract.

Each term you are at New College you will join with a faculty member (called your *sponsor*) to design a program of activities for that term. The *contract* is the document which describes the program the two of you desire. At the end of the term your academic standing will be determined by your success at fulfilling the term's contract. Nine successfully completed contracts are normally required for the B.A. College work done prior to matriculation at New College can be considered for credit toward the degree, thereby reducing the number of contracts required.

YOUR FIRST CONTRACT AT NEW COLLEGE

First, take a candid look at yourself. Contrary to what you may feel when you arrive on campus and enter a world of strangers, you are here because you have many qualities which you can affirm and use.

Much of your exploration and involvement will have an "ad hoc" quality as you set out to create a first term's contract. You will stumble upon resources, happen to meet people who can respond to you, be surprised to find an interest you never knew you had. But the college community does not rely solely on chance; several structures and services exist to help you arrange the contract.

Your *orientation advisor* is a member of the faculty or administrative staff who is specifically designated to be available to you and a small group of your fellow students during the first days of the term. He or she will talk with you about ways your interests and goals can be developed through your academic program. The orientation advisor is available as you proceed through your initial formulation of educational goals and can help you identify a potential sponsor for your contract. The *Dean of Student Affairs* and his assistants will be deeply involved in orienting you to campus life during the first weeks. They are ready to aid you with housing problems, obtaining recreational resources, putting on a social function, identifying resources in town, etc. In addition to serving as general resource people, the Dean of Student Affairs and his assistants, as well as the faculty members residing on campus, are available in personal emergencies. The *College Recorder's Office* is the repository for all academic records including your own. The *Recorder* can help if you have questions about the mechanics of the curriculum and your record. The *Off-Campus Study Office* can help you identify field study resources to be used in the future. Two *course lists,* one for the term you are about to begin and one for the entire academic year, tell what courses faculty plan to offer.

The *Human Resources Guide,* which contains profiles of faculty and staff, will help you know the people in this community, as they describe themselves. Read the *Guide* thoroughly. You will find, for example, that many of us have interests not usually associated with our professional fields. With a personal commitment to explore and thoroughly use the above resources, you will have a sound basis for finding a contract sponsor and creating your first contract.

YOUR CONTRACT SPONSOR

Your initial explorations should enable you to identify interests and goals which will shape your academic activities for the coming months. Particular interests and goals will in turn suggest a specific faculty member as a potential contract *sponsor.*

Discussion between you and a potential sponsor might be viewed as a process of negotiation. The faculty member will have views on what constitutes valid educational endeavor and what skills you need to achieve the ends you propose. You will have your own views on these matters and out of the dialogue can come a mutual understanding about a contract—a decision to make a commitment and put it into writing, to alter goals, or perhaps to search elsewhere, with other faculty.

Once a contract is negotiated, the sponsor becomes the focal point of your various educational activities. With your sponsor you have the opportunity to develop themes from disparate events, plan for the future, assess the past.

WRITING UP THE CONTRACT

The contract has four basic parts: Goals, Educational Activities,

Descriptions, and Certification Criteria. Below are some guidelines for filling out each part. A sample contract blank is included to aid you in following this discussion.

Goals

This part of your contract is intended to give an overview and unifying theme for your contract. In it you should state long- and short-range goals, indicating how the term's activities relate to both types of goal. For example, a long-range goal underlying your work might be to have a career in medicine. A short-range goal for a term or series of terms would be to master certain bodies of knowledge which are prerequisite to a medical career. To this end, work in, say, organic chemistry would be included in the term's contract. Not all goals can be so readily expressed in academic terminology as the example just given.

Educational Activities

This section is for listing the particular activities you intend to pursue as means for attaining your formal academic goals. Because most of the activities you list will be recorded on your transcript by the Recorder, it is important that you understand this section clearly. If in doubt about a particular listing, consult your faculty sponsor and the Recorder. It is very important to differentiate (in the contract) between activities that you are engaging in *for transcript entry* and those which are an important part of your overall program for the term but are not to be entered on a transcript. Only activities planned with and evaluated by New College faculty members will be entered on your transcript. Such activities may be any combination of courses, tutorials, laboratories, field work, and special projects. The course list announces courses and laboratories in advance of the term in which they are offered.

Satisfactory completion of a course, laboratory, or tutorial means that through your work you have met the instructor's performance standards. The instructor will submit an evaluation of your work at the end of the term. Most evaluations comment on the substance of the work to aid you in assessing your academic competence.

In some instances special projects will not be intended for evaluation and eventual transcript listing. Perhaps no faculty member is competent to evaluate the performance involved, or perhaps the activity is highly subjective in nature and an observer's comments are not appropriate. The reason for listing such activities on the contract at all is simply to recognize that they are part of your educational program.

Descriptions And Other Activities

This section is to allow for further elaboration and description of the activities listed above for transcript entry. Normally entries such as courses, laboratories, etc. do not need further description; however, tutorials and especially special projects may require further description. Also, here you may list projects and activities that you are not undertaking for transcript entry but which you and your sponsor consider an important part of your term's study. Activities such as "singing in a madrigal group" and "helping register voters" are examples of endeavors you might wish to note on your contract but which you and your sponsor might not consider part of your formal education.

Certification Criteria

You and your sponsor have complete autonomy over selection of your educational activities and procedures for evaluating your contract. This section of the contract is where you spell out in detail the criteria for satisfactory completion of the contract. The certification criteria for a given contract might be quite simple. For example, they might be satisfactory completion of several or all of a group of seminars you have listed. In that case you have only to attain satisfactory performances as certified by evaluations from the instructors involved. But a contract consists of goals to be accomplished as well as seminars to be completed and you may want the certification criteria to reflect this. When the criteria for completing a contract are other (or more) than satisfactory completion of a group of faculty-supervised activities, you and your sponsor must be careful to avoid misunderstanding.

CONTRACT CERTIFICATION

At the end of the term your contract sponsor will determine the status of your contract according to the certification criteria you (both) agreed upon at the outset. In the simplest cases, all the sponsor need do is verify that you have achieved the requisite "satisfactories" in the term's activities. In instances where the criteria for certification are less clear-cut, the sponsor will refer to the conferences you and he/she have had during the term. In every instance you should request a term's end conference with your sponsor to review your progress to date and plan for following terms. Based on the evidence of term's work submitted to her/him, the sponsor will select from three mutually exclusive categories to describe your contract's status: *satisfactory, incomplete,* and *unsatisfactory.* The first means that you have been judged as having met the obligations to which you originally committed yourself.The second, "incomplete," means that you have completed some of the obligations successfully, but not all. When the unfulfilled portions are completed acording to a schedule you and the sponsor devise, the status of the contract can be shifted by the sponsor to "satisfactory." However, *a contract not completed within one calendar year from the beginning of the term for which the contract was written becomes unsatisfactory.* Finally, if your sponsor determines that your work is inadequate in major respects and correction of the deficiencies unlikely or educationally unprofitable, your contract will be called "unsatisfactory."

The future is free and open. We look forward
to a year of life, of struggle and of joy.

At the time the educational contract was adopted as the central curricular device at New College, it was expected that fundamental changes would result in the College's academic program. This expectation was based on the fact that the newly developed contract system was both "open and "pure." It was "open" in the sense that no restrictions existed with respect to either contract design or content; and it was "pure" in the sense that no curriculum committee or administrator could veto a contract or intervene in any way between individual student and individual sponsor.

In an "open" and "pure" contract system of education such as the one at New College, one might expect considerable variety among student contracts. As we have stated above, the variety has been less than was anticipated. Nevertheless, interesting differences do exist. In order to highlight these differences and in order to clarify further what contracting at New College means, we are reproducing here sample contracts. To insure anonymity we have deleted all data which might have served to identify either student or contract sponsor. Furthermore, for analytical purposes we have organized the examples according to types. We do not intend to suggest that this typology is exhaustive nor that all or most contracts would fit neatly into it. Hopefully, by organizing the sample contracts in this manner the variety that is possible in the New College system will become apparent. The seven types which we have isolated are: the Survey Contract; the Methodological Contract; the Thematic Contract; the Research Contract; the Skill Contract; the "Applied" Contract; and the Off-Campus Study Contract. (For their assistance in preparing these samples, the authors wish to express their appreciation to Dr. Dru Dougherty and Dr. Patalie Rosel.)

The manifest consequences of two years' experience with the contract system have been less dramatic than anyone expected. In particular, this has been the case in the areas of program design, teaching techniques, student-faculty interaction, admissions patterns, and student attrition. The area where drama was most expected, but where it has been barely apparent, is in individual program design. To be sure, the contract system encourages students to integrate more coherently their curricular and extra-curricular activities in relation to educational and career goals. Nevertheless, program design is, for the most part, highly conventional even though the specific subject matter incorporated into the contract may vary widely. The possibility for such variety does not derive from the unique features of the contract system, however, but rather from a low student-faculty ratio which allows for tutorials and independent reading programs or study projects. The simple fact is that a majority of contracts consist of a collection of three, four or more formal courses related to relatively amorphous, short-run goals, with passing work in the individual courses as the primary criterion of success. During Fall Term, academic year 1973-74, for example, 303 contracts out of a total 489 contracts (62%) were basically of this type. Only 5% of the contracts (24) required a self-evaluation from the student as part of the certification criteria. This figure is interesting in light of the fact that the contract system was adopted, in part, because it was viewed as a predominantly "student-centered" curricular device. In general, the contract mechanism simply has not generated the self-reflection about or the inventiveness with respect to program design that was anti-

CONTRACT

OFF-CAMPUS STUDY CONTRACT

Academic Year 1973-74, Term _____

NEW COLLEGE
SARASOTA, FLORIDA 33578

UBRAN LIFE TERM IN HOBOKEN, NEW JERSEY

☐ On-Campus
☒ Off-Campus
Study

Campus
Box
No. _____

NAME _____
(Please print or type)

Goals:

To enable each student to better understand the qualities and problems
of traditional urban life and, more broadly, to expand personal competence
and consciousness by undertaking research and service obligations in a culture
different from those we are most experienced in. Toward these basic goals
students will employ team research and sharing of urban experience along with
the individual activities conventionally involved in a field experience term.

Educational Activities to be evaluated for transcript entry: Instructor/Evaluator

Please have
applicable
faculty mem-
bers initial
the following:
Tutorials,
Fieldwork,
Spec. Projects

1. Internship with an agency or group
    providing some service in and to Hoboken.

2. Team research project on some aspect of
    Hoboken life.*

3. "Empathic study" of a Hoboken person,
    family, work group or the like

Descriptions and Other Activities:

Other activities: Homestay with a Hoboken area family. Participation in weekly meetings of
New College group, some of which will be focused around topics selected in advance of the
meetings by participants and taped for use at New College. Descriptions: (1) Undertake
obligations with community group or agency. One or both of two thrusts will probably develop
undertake an action project for which student has major responsibility and see it through to
completion, or carry out a research project providing significant analysis of some aspect of
the group's functioning or plans. (2) Study of urban life carried out as a team effort by
program participants. (3) Study of a person's or "natural group's" lifestyle and the forces
which shape it. The student will project him/herself into the situation of the subject and
try to understand the subject's behavior in the subject's terms.

**Certification
Criteria:**

Satisfactory completion of the above-listed "transcript" activities; successful carrying
through of a home-stay for the term; participation in the group meetings to satisfaction
of the group. There will be a discussion of the term's accomplishments, problems, benefits
involving participants and sponsors at end of term.

Student Signature _____   Date _____

Sponsor Signature _____   Date _____

Consultant (when applicable) _____ Date _____
The team, not the individual student, will be evaluated. Team evaluation will apply to all te
members without differentiation.
Please return complete set to Recorder's Office

CONTRACT

THEMATIC CONTRACT

Academic Year 1973-74, Term _____

NEW COLLEGE
SARASOTA, FLORIDA 39578

☒ **On-Campus**
☐ **Off-Campus**
Study

Campus
Box
No. _____

NAME _____
(Please print or type)

Goals:

I wish to continue my study of Latin America this term. My approach will concentrate
on an anthropological approach as well as on the language and literature of the area.

I will also continue my interest in language and language learning: learning a new
language and teaching two others, as well as studying language from a theoretical
viewpoint.

Educational Activities to be evaluated for transcript entry: Instructor/Evaluator

**Please have
applicable
faculty mem-
bers initial
the following:
Tutorials,
Fieldwork,
Spec. Projects**

Methods in Cultural Anthropology
Latin America (Anthropology)
Women in Latin America
Latin American Literature
Romantics: English Poets
Beginning Portuguese
Fieldwork in Bilingual Education
Seminar in Linguistics (non-credit)
Tutoring in Spanish

Descriptions and Other Activities:

Women in Latin America will be a study of the role of women in that area. Readings
will include a theoretical treatment of sex roles as well as individual readings
on various women, groups, and countries.

Latin American Literature will be a survey of the literature with special emphasis
on trends in literature in general.

Beginning Portuguese will be done independently using Modern Portuguese (PLDG)
and accompanying tapes. A minimum of 3 hours per week will be spent in the lab.
Fieldwork will be an extension of last term's activities.

Certification
Criteria:

This contract will be judged satisfactory by mutual consent of the contract
sponsor and the student, using individual course evaluations as a basis.

Student Signature _____   **Date** _____

Sponsor Signature _____   **Date** _____

Consultant (when applicable) _____   **Date** _____

Please return complete set to Recorder's Office

RESEARCH CONTRACT   **CONTRACT**

NEW COLLEGE   Academic Year 1973-74, Term _____
SARASOTA, FLORIDA 33578
NAME _____
(Please print or type)

☒   **On-Campus**
☐   **Off-Campus**
          Study

Campus
Box
No. _____

Goals:

> To develop a full understanding of x-ray crystallography and to
>
> solve a crystal structure.

Educational Activities to be evaluated for transcript entry:

Instructor/Evaluator

Please have
applicable
faculty mem-
bers initial
the following:
Tutorials,
Fieldwork,
Spec. Projects

Crystal Structure Analysis
Crystallographic Computer Programming
Readings in Crystallographic Theory
Research in Inorganic Chemistry

Descriptions and Other Activities:

> Four tutorials with a member of the chemistry faculty. I will be working
> to achieve the above stated goals and to establish on-campus facilities
> for the solution of crystal structures.

Certification
Criteria:

> Satisfactory completion of above to be determined by my research sponsor.

Student Signature _____   Date _____

Sponsor Signature _____   Date _____

Consultant (when applicable) _____   Date _____

Please return complete set to Recorder's Office

SURVEY CONTRACT

CONTRACT

NEW COLLEGE
SARASOTA, FLORIDA 33578

Academic Year 1973-74, Term _____

☒ On-Campus
☐ Off-Campus
  Study

NAME _____
(Please print or type)

Campus
Box
No. _____

Goals:

To gain a better basic understanding of many areas of study, and therefore

attempt to identify my main areas of interest.

Educational Activities to be evaluated for transcript entry:

Instructor/Evaluator

Please have
applicable
faculty mem-
bers initial
the following:
Tutorials,
Fieldwork,
Spec. Projects

Intro. Biology II
Intro. Biology Lab
Human Economics
Intro. to Social Psychology
Social and Political Philosophy
Philosophy of Psychology
A Study of War - Audit

Descriptions and Other Activities:

Ballet twice a week (2 hours); jewelry-making twice a week (5 hours);

daily flute practice sessions; ceramics.

Certification
Criteria:

To complete successfully at least four courses.

Student Signature _____ **Date** _____
Sponsor Signature _____ **Date** _____
Consultant (when applicable) _____ **Date** _____

Please return complete set to Recorder's Office

CONTRACT

METHODOLOGICAL CONTRACT

Academic Year 1973-74, Term _____

NEW COLLEGE
SARASOTA, FLORIDA 33578

☒ **On-Campus**
☐ **Off-Campus**
          Study

Campus
Box
No. _____

NAME _____
(Please print or type)

Goals:
As there are only two terms left to my stay at New College, in the time
remaining I hope to get experience and knowledge in those areas of
biology which I expect to be relevant to my future work in animal
behavior. My goals this term are to study, learn and perform the
techniques and methods involved in describing as many aspects of an eco-
system as feasible in a term's time, so as to apply eventually the data
to a particular problem or problems.

Educational Activities to be evaluated for transcript entry: Instructor/Evaluator

Please have
applicable
faculty mem-
bers initial
the following:
Tutorials,
Fieldwork,
Spec. Projects

Bird identification and census.
Determination of mammal population and density.
Determination of composition and relative density
   of terrestial invertebrates, including use of
   appropriate biological keys.
Study of life histories of selected animals from
   above studies.
General knowledge of methods of vegetation and
   soil analysis.

Descriptions and Other Activities:

These studies will be performed on groups of islands in the Sarasota vicinity.
Bird studies will include a count of the number of species seen, number of
individuals of each species and the activities the birds engage in. Mammal
study will be done with a grid system and capture-recapture techniques. Invertebrate
study will include flying, crawling and soil organisms, using a variety of methods.
Knowledge of vegetation and soil analysis, as well as other physico-chemical
aspects of the environment, will come from working with people studying these
areas, assisting them whenever possible.

Certification
Criteria:

Certification will be based on competence in techniques and methods learned
in all areas of the study and the kind and amount of knowledge acquired in the
study. These will be judged by a critical self-evaluation and by discussions
with my contract sponsor.

Student Signature _____   Date _____

Sponsor Signature _____   Date _____

Consultant (when applicable) _____   Date _____

Please return complete set to Recorder's Office

SKILL CONTRACT

NEW COLLEGE
SARASOTA, FLORIDA 33578

CONTRACT

Academic Year 1973-74, Term _____

☒ **On-Campus**
☐ **Off-Campus**
   Study

Campus
Box
No. _____

NAME _____
(Please print or type)

Goals:

I would like to become proficient at several classical languages. I also
want to study ancient cultures and their arts. I believe that these
foundations will assist me in a career in Archaeology, the field of my
primary interest. During this term, I intend to remain active in both
on- and off-campus activities as well as academic studies.

Educational Activities to be evaluated for transcript entry:

Instructor/Evaluator

Please have
applicable
faculty mem-
bers initial
the following:
Tutorials,
Fieldwork,
Spec. Projects

Intermediate Greek
Latin
The Ancient Mediterranean
Medieval Music
Creative Drawing I: Point/Line

Descriptions and Other Activities:

During this period, I intend to do considerable reading in archaeology.
At the end of the term I will present an annotated bibliography to my sponsor,
listing the reading that I have done. This term I will also continue with
my job at the Sarasota Boys' Club as an art instructor. I will also be a
sailing instructor on campus. The Latin tutorial will enable me to review
my high school Latin and progress into more advanced work.

Certification
Criteria:

In order to obtain a satisfactory contract evaluation I will complete four
out of five courses in a satisfactory manner.

Student Signature _____   **Date** _____

Sponsor Signature _____   **Date** _____

Consultant (when applicable) _____   **Date** _____

Please return complete set to Recorder's Office

CONTRACT

"APPLIED" CONTRACT

Academic Year 1973-74, Term _____

☐ **On-Campus**
☐ **Off-Campus**
    Study

NEW COLLEGE
SARASOTA, FLORIDA 33578

Campus
Box
No. _____

NAME _____
(Please print or type)

Goals:

This term I intend to examine several different aspects of political science.
My major concern is campaigning for the Constitutional Convention in
New Hampshire. Whatever the results, I hope that this experience will help me
in preparing for my campaign for the New Hampshire legislature. [In order
that this goal not appear unrealistic, the authors wish to point out that one
New College student, Stephen Dupree, was successful in his bid for the
New Hampshire legislature.]

Educational Activities to be evaluated for transcript entry: Instructor/Evaluator

Please have
applicable
faculty mem-
bers initial
the following:
Tutorials,
Fieldwork,
Spec. Projects

Revising the Constitution
Public Opinion
Tutorial: The Kennedy Administration
Special Project: Campaigning for the
Constitutional Convention in New Hampshire*

Descriptions and Other Activities:

*This will involve going to New Hampshire for two weeks and campaigning until
the election, March 5th. I will report to my sponsor upon my return on my
experiences.

I will be working 15 hours a week as a waitress.

I will be, independently, improving my photographic skills.

Certification
Criteria:

Satisfactory completion of three courses and the campaign.

Student Signature _____   Date _____

Sponsor Signature _____   Date _____

Consultant (when applicable) _____   Date _____

Please return complete set to Recorder's Office

cipated. It could be that the faculty were not well trained in the use of contracts outside of courses.

In the area of teaching techniques there has been as little drama as in that of program design. The contract curriculum has yet to stimulate any radical innovation—with one exception—in the way the disciplines are taught. Most campus work is done through lecture-discussion courses, seminars, tutorials, and independent study. All of these modes were in widespread use toward the same pedagogical ends prior to the adoption of the contract system.

Exception to the above pattern has occurred in the social sciences and biology where cross-cultural and field studies now play an important role. The contract system, we have found, facilitates the design of field-based projects and their incorporation into the formal academic program. Although possibly part of a national trend, as a result, students in political science, sociology, anthropology, social psychology, and biology in the New College program increasingly use cross-cultural experience and field research as tools of study. This is in marked contrast to the earlier, more conventional curricular structure which tended either to discourage field-based projects or to force them into inappropriate molds designed for classroom activities.

The conventionality of contract design and pedagogical techniques under the contract system confirms perhaps the survival potential of the traditional disciplines (including the languages which are well enrolled) in a structure lacking external compulsion. This should be reassuring to those who fear that traditional, widely validated academic activities can only prosper if some formal force, however benign, imposes them on the individual. The same outcome will probably not be reassuring, however, to those who think that conventional curricular rules have been the primary impediments to creative student and faculty activity.

Student-faculty interaction, always considered an important dimension of life at a residential, liberal arts college, does not seem to be altered substantially by the new curriculum. Now, as well as in the early years of the College, the same variety of interaction patterns—some intimate; some distant and aloof—have been observed. This is disquieting because the student-contract sponsor relationship is much more central to the success of the contract curriculum than the student-academic advisor relationship is for a traditional curriculum. In the absence of institutional constraints, a contract system is wholly dependent upon the quality of student-faculty interaction for maintaining a college's claim to program coherence and academic excellence. If the quality of this interaction is marginal, students can, with ease, become casual dilettantes or narrowly trained specialists. While neither extreme has become the pattern at New College, we are concerned with the tendency of a "pure" contract system to move in these directions. There have been, for example, sufficient cases to cause concern of students' going through much of their college careers without articulating long-term goals, shifting from area to area, and avoiding focus in their programs of study. At an opposite extreme faculty members can, and often do, permit students to concentrate excessively in a given discipline or a limited number of disciplines. Thus, we presently have an example of two students with a combined total of eleven academic terms who have completed successfully 37 courses in mathematics and only 8 courses outside this discipline. While these two students provide extreme examples, the phenomenon in question occurs most often in the humanities, not the sciences. The contract system alone would appear, therefore, to be an inadequate response to the "two cultures" problem.

Finally, innovators generally look to curricular changes to affect a college's admissions and attrition patterns, placing the college in a more competitive admissions position and yielding a better retention rate. Although a two-year period is too brief to allow for definitive claims, it would appear that New College's shift from a relatively traditional curriculum to the contract system has not had dramatic consequences in these two areas. As the College's reputation for academic excellence became established in the late 1960s and accreditation was earned in record time, the pool of applicants expanded rapidly. Although a peak in the number of applicants seems to have been reached in the past two or three years, there has not been a dropoff in applicants parallel to that affecting many other liberal arts institutions. Perhaps this is due to the adoption of the contract system. Admissions interview data indicate, however, that even under the early curricular structure the College's emphases on academic excellence and individualized instruction were paramount in drawing students.

Attrition over the past five years has been virtually unchanged, although there seems to be a process of redistribution. Freshman attrition is declining, whereas upperclass attrition has increased. Once again, the time-frame in which the contract system has been in operation is too short to permit confident explanations. A promising hypothesis, however, is suggested by a point made earlier—namely, the facilitation of field experience education afforded by the contract system. By allowing non-classroom activities to be included in their academic programs, the educational contract makes it possible for the academically uncommitted to realize that there are more supportive environments for their interests than institutions of formal education. In such cases, withdrawal is eventually chosen. A contract system, therefore, does not curtail leave taking; it merely delays it. We will, of course, be interested in testing further this hypothesis in the next several years.

In summation, the point to be stressed is that the contract system at New College has not introduced radical changes. It is not the path to a new philistinism—an unleashing of the counter-culture—as some have predicted. At the same time, it is not a means for releasing heretofore suppressed student genius which will usher in an educational utopia.*

Since educators place so much emphasis on the curriculum, it is important that an attempt be made to explain why New College has experienced a lack of drama, why so substantial a change has failed so far to produce greater overall change. The key to such an explanation, we believe, is the fact that curricular structure, per se, does not impinge directly on the primary forces affecting educational processes. Furthermore, the contract system, while a response to the erosion of traditional curricular authority, shows limited promise with respect to mobilizing any alternative kinds of authority. This limitation makes it difficult for a contract system by itself to influence the manner in which professors organize their

---

*For expectations along these contrasting lines see Sidney Hook, "John Dewey and His Betrayers," *Change Magazine,* Vol. 7 (November 1971), 22-26; and Alan Waterman, "Learning by Contract," *Change Magazine,* Vol. 8 (Winter 1972-3), 12ff.

disciplines, teach their specialties, and relate to students as well as to affect the decision of a student to enroll at a particular college or to remain at the institution. If we look at each area where substantial change was expected, the above points can be made in more concrete terms.

PROGRAM DESIGN AND TEACHING TECHNIQUES. As has been noted, the "open" and "pure" form of New College's contract system permits maximum flexibility with respect to program design and teaching techniques. Theoretical options, however, do not necessarily stimulate students or faculty to experiment, to use new resources, or to engage in new learning modes. Futhermore, only on rare occasions does an undergraduate curriculum reorganize bodies of knowledge or identify new intellectual territory. (Possible examples of such occasions are the University of Chicago syllabus which introduced the social sciences and Columbia University's General Education Program.) In general, a curricular structure is not the creator of academic subject matter but rather the embodiment of pre-existing subject matter. Consequently, one has to look at forces other than curricular devices in order to determine what is most likely to affect teaching techniques and the content of students' programs of study. Among the most obvious forces are requirements for entry into graduate and professional schools, the schooling received by faculty members in graduate centers, scholarly interests of faculty as shaped by funding possibilities, and the organizational structure of the various disciplines at given points in time.

Although our discussion has focused on the "contract-based curriculum" at New College, the actual structure and content of programs of study depend on the individual faculty members who shape and give legitimacy to a student's program, not on the contract system itself nor the institution. New College's faculty, like that of many other institutions, received their Ph.D.s from elite graduate centers where they were schooled to think of their disciplines as comprised of specific sub-fields and organized along traditional lines, and where they were prepared to teach standard courses such as organic chemistry, epistemology, the French Revolution, macro-economics, etc. In addition, through their own research and publications they have contributed to the survival potential of these very structures. It should come as no surprise, therefore, that the New College faculty has utilized to such a limited degree the learning contract's flexibility for developing new ways to organize material or to disseminate knowledge. To have done so would have been itself a cause for surprise.

Given the centrality of the faculty to a contract system of education and given the forces that shape the scholarly interests and pedagogical values of a faculty, a mere change in curricular structure can hardly be expected to have far-reaching effects. This is particularly the case when the curricular structure in question does not impose any new models of learning or of problem solving, but is instead an open-ended registration form which is given substance by the collection of course offerings and other resources made available by the faculty of the College. Far from being a revolutionary development, the educational contract can be a highly conservative structure in that it allows existing staff priorities, disciplinary values, and faculty alliances to persist unconstrained. A contract system of education cannot force new learning priorities or new forms of student-faculty interaction.

STUDENT-FACULTY INTERACTION. An avant-garde curriculum does not affect dramatically the fundamental conditions of student-faculty relationships because it cannot overcome the fact that students and faculty move in substantially different worlds. Age, experience, family status, education, career status, knowledge—these as well as other factors separate faculty and students; and it is well that they do, for the whole concept of schooling which is an essential ingredient in formal education is based on faculty-student disparity in these areas.

In a contract system of education the faculty, with its specialized expertise, still seems imposing and somewhat mysterious to students, regardless of the close relationships that may develop between student and sponsor. Each group's expectations for and assumptions about the other contain numerous disparities stemming from differing perceptions, priorities, needs, and experiences. No curricular structure, we suspect, can overcome entirely, or even significantly restructure, these differences. In fact, a contract system, depending as heavily as it does on student-sponsor interaction, may reveal them as threatening even more than a conventional curriculum which builds rituals around the differences.

A total contract system such as the one at New College places a premium on the quality of student-sponsor interaction and, in turn, on the quality of the faculty. Recruitment activity and retention decisions take on an even greater significance than in colleges with traditional curricula. In addition to the usual professional skills, a candidate must have such personal traits as: a tolerance for ambiguity and uncertainty; sufficient "ego strength" to demand work of high quality from students when institutional constraints are at a minimum; and a system of values which provides a basis for distinguishing momentary fads from what possesses lasting educational merit. In the absence of an officially sanctioned curriculum, the integrity of the institution is wholly dependent upon the presence of such qualities among its faculty. Any college which is considering the adoption of a contract system would be well advised to take this fact with the utmost seriousness.

ADMISSIONS AND ATTRITION. Although educators seem inclined to believe otherwise, it is likely that specific curricular structures have little to do with a student's choice of a college. In addition to obvious factors such as cost, location, religious preference, parental prohibitions and incentives, it is the general image of a college which affects selection activity. Most new matriculants know little about the specifics of an institution's curriculum, even though they do have a definite image of the school (not necessarily an accurate one, of course). As has already been noted, admissions data at New College indicate that such adjectives and phrases as "experimental," "individualized," "academic excellence," and "concerned faculty" figure most prominently in the minds of applicants. This is the case under the present contract system, but it was also true when the curriculum adhered to a traditional, liberal arts model.

It is a commonplace that the military draft, or the lack thereof, has far more to do with attrition patterns than does the curriculum. Family pressures, financial conditions, the job market, and youth-culture trends also have significant impact, and all of these are relatively, if not completely, independent of curricular considerations. To be sure, a contract system may keep some students enrolled who otherwise would drop out due to the possibility of receiving academic credit for off-campus activities. This advantage, however, is accompanied (as we have seen) by the risk that the academically uncommitted student will discover in off-campus work more appealing environments than a college campus. Rather than reduce the attrition rate, a contract system may, at best, merely redistribute it. This, at least, appears to be the case at New College over the past two years.

Although the many negative aspects of the use of the contract system need to be understood and noted, New College's two-year involvement with a contract system suggests that this curricular device, through its flexibility and potential responsiveness to student interests, does ameliorate some of the problems associated with traditional curricula. In particular, students look upon their educational experience as more meaningful in personal terms as a result of participating in the design of their programs of study. Opportunities for independent research projects during academic terms are increased, and the College has been rescued from the myopia which comes from thinking that the classroom exhausts the educational universe. Finally, the contract system (even with its limitations) does provide a mechanism which supports the activity of faculty who are inclined to explore new ways to organize and to present their disciplines. For these, and other, reasons New College continues to be optimistic about the educational contract. The problems associated with a contract system which have been raised in this discussion are not viewed as causes for discouragement. To the contrary, we believe that our two-year experience has given us a more realistic perspective from which to assess the educational potential of this curricular device. This perspective has been gained by confronting directly the learning contract's limitations. The contract system of education is not a panacea. To have learned in specific terms why this is not the case permits New College to make a modest contribution to the ongoing assessment of a potentially significant educational reform.

We began this review of New College's experience with the contract system by noting its relation to the decline of curricular authority presently occurring in American higher education. In conclusion, we wish to return to this theme and to underscore what has been implicit throughout—namely, the limited capacity of the contract system to redeem the loss of authority. Whatever its other strengths may be, the contract's relationship to the loss of collegiate authority is problematical.

Two lines of argument have been developed to support the above conclusion. The first is that an undergraduate curriculum—whatever its structure—is peripheral to the major forces which shape the dynamics of a college and, as such, is relatively impotent to affect the educational process. Second, and more important, is the laissez-faire nature of the contract, which allows students and faculty members to design programs of study more-or-less as they desire. In the final analysis, this characteristic of the contract system mitigates against the development of a stable new authority. The actions of individuals within a contract curriculum are precisely that—the actions of individuals. They are not selectively validated or idealized by the institution so as to become authoritative. Thus, the institution's growing inability to prescribe directly and confidently, which we discussed at the outset, is only confirmed by the contract system. In effect, the contract admits that the College is not able to say through its curriculum: "This is relevant knowledge; this is not. This we offer here; this we do not offer."

To the extent that the decline of collegiate authority is a major problem for undergraduate institutions, the contract curriculum may undermine rather than revitalize the liberal arts college's position. Once the individualistic ethic of the contract system is accepted—that is, do your own thing so long as resources are available—it is only a short move to the question: "why have a curriculum at all?" The student might fare better financially and equally well intellectually simply by purchasing learning resources on the open market—a correspondence course here; a lecture series there. The only missing ingredient would be the degree credit.

POSTSCRIPT

Since the thrust of the present volume is practical as well as interpretative-analytical, we would like to add, in the manner of a coda, a number of "points to ponder" for those who might be considering the adoption of a contract-based curriculum. We place these observations in a "Postscript" not because we consider them unimportant but because we want the foregoing interpretation and assessment to stand independently as a basis for thought about contract systems of education regardless of the techniques employed in implementing such systems. Among the more important practical considerations to keep in mind are:

1. The contract-based curriculum is not a panacea. It does not magically produce student commitment where there has been none; imaginative teaching where this has been lacking; intimate student-faculty interaction where perfunctory advising has been standard procedure; or increased admissions applications or better retention statistics where these have been on the decline. New College's experience suggests that a contract system of education may free creative minds; it does not create creativity.

2. People are everything. As platitudinous as this statement may appear, those who are considering the adoption of a contract system are advised to take it quite seriously. As we have argued above, a contract system of education, rather than introducing a new form of institutional authority, shifts authority with respect to curricular matters to individuals, in particular to individual members of the faculty. This shift is most apparent in such areas as the designing of students' programs of study and the maintenance of quality controls within the educational program. Consequently, the nature of a faculty's strengths and weaknesses is all important. If an administrator or department chairman has doubts about his faculty's ability to perform in the absence of institutionally sanctioned support mechanisms, he should question the contract's suitability for his institution.

3. A contractual system of education requires a broader range of faculty competence than a more traditional curriculum. In such a system a professor's responsibility extends beyond research, publication, and classroom instruction into the areas of program design, new forms of academic counseling, and the evaluation of non-classroom learning (e. g., field internships and cross-cultural experiences). For many faculty members these activities will represent novel demands for which they have received little or no training. Accompanying the new demands are difficult questions about judging faculty competence. Who is to evaluate faculty performance in the new areas of responsibility and by what criteria? What weight is to be given to competence in these areas in relation to research and publication, classroom teaching, and committee

work? Clearly, these are not unanswerable questions, but they require open discussion, and a faculty must be forewarned as to the increased range of obligations it will be assuming in a contract system.

4. In a college or university where there is a lack of consensus as to the institution's basic purpose(s), the laissez-faire nature of a contract system may bring into the open irreconcilable dissension. Is the goal of the institution to provide a "liberal arts" education or preprofessional training; should the university be an agent of social change or a place for objective, dispassionate inquiry; is individual self-discovery through creative expression the aim of education or the mastery of institutional disciplines? A contract system of education may not be a helpful curricular framework within which to decide questions such as these. The point, once again, is that unless an institution can tolerate the pluralism which a contract system encourages, serious thought should be given to its suitabiliy for that institution.

5. A virtue of the contract system of education is that, in spite of its being a potentially revolutionary curricular device, it can be relatively inexpensive (in terms of both time and money) to implement. New College developed its program in approximately six months with a grant of less than $10,000 proving sufficient to cover special staff and related costs. Futhermore, a variety of models for contract programs has already been developed. New College, for example, has developed one such model for a residential "liberal arts" college, and New York's Empire State College has developed yet another model for an external degree program. In contrast, therefore, to general education programs which must develop fully articulated core courses before being launched, it is possible to begin a contract program with a limited amount of valuable faculty and administrative planning time.

6. Although start-up costs for a contract program can be relatively low, there are costs, unique to the contract system, which are required after implementation. Certain administrative expenses in a contract program may prove higher than in the case of a conventional curriculum. For example, student academic records are more complex when they involve contracts and narrative evaluations than when they consist of course registrations and traditional

grades. Consequently, one can expect that the registrar's office will require both an expanded staff and a new records system. The cost implications of adopting a contract system combined with a non-traditional grading system (such as exists at New College) extends beyond the registrar's office. In particular, the amount of administrative and faculty time required for the review of students in academic difficulty is considerable. To individualize undergraduate education through contract learning is also to individualize the review process. At New College, for instance, no other faculty committee approaches the time demands required by the Student Academic Status Committee, the body which monitors the individual performance of students. A third and final example of a cost unique to a contract curriculum is related to the need for special support systems. One such system is an ongoing program of workshops or training seminars in techniques for effective academic counseling. As we have argued above, the quality of counseling received in the student-contract sponsor relationship is much more central to the success of the contract curriculum than the student-academic advisor relationship is for a traditional curriculum.

7. Finally, a contractual curriculum tends toward solipsism. Common educational experiences are a rarity; the pursuit of individual goals is the rule. A college considering the adoption of a contract system will need to reinforce its supportive, communal, "nurturing" services if a humane environment conducive to learning, however individualized, is to be maintained.

5 ARTHUR CHICKERING

Developing Intellectual Competence at Empire State

Empire State College operates through a series of geographically separated learning centers located throughout the State of New York. Students receive counseling on admission prior to articulating their Degree Program, which describes their purposes and the learning activities they will undertake to achieve those purposes. This program, which includes information about competence, knowledge, and personal development achieved prior to enrollment, is submitted to a faculty committee for approval. When approved it becomes the general framework within which individual learning contracts are pursued.

In a contract the mentor and student describe plans for learning in more detail than does a typical professor in a conventional college course, and the mentor designs a much larger part of the student's studies than does a single faculty member in a conventional college university department.

Because mentors are called upon to advise students outside their specific area of competence, they need to turn to other resources. These resources may range widely, such as Empire State College

---

[1]The initial portion of this paper concerning various dimensions of intellectual competence, was prepared in the main by John McCormick. The latter draws on a report from the Research and Evaluation Staff, Ernest Palola, Assistant Vice-President for Research and Evaluation, Timothy Lehmann, Director of Program Evaluation, Paul Bradley, Director of Institutional Research, and Dick Debus, Director of Cost Analysis, and was prepared with the help of Outcomes Committee members Laurence Lipsett, Lloyd Lill, and Jerry Thomas.

learning programs, SUNY independent study courses, supervised field and work experiences, courses at other colleges and by associations and corporations, correspondence courses, museum programs, and some proprietary school offerings.

INTELLECTUAL COMPETENCE

The most common educational goal of most colleges and universities is the development of intellectual competence or intellectual skills. Improved intellectual skills can help a student become a problem solver, a manager of his own existence, and a learner who is learning how to learn. The educator's role is to deliberately bring such skills to the student and thus expand the student's competence. Intellectual skills then become internalized and functional as problem-solving tools. All this is simply one way of saying that the objectives of Empire State College are not centered on knowledge for the sake of knowledge. Rather, intellectual skills are important because they increase the capacity of the individual to manage his or her own affairs and to operate effectively in chosen endeavors.

If the mentor is to help students move through experiences that are deliberately designed to increase intellectual skills, specificity about what those skills involve and how they can be implemented in learning contracts is necessary.

Bloom and others (1956) identify and define knowledge and then proceed to outline five intellectual skills: comprehension, application, analysis, synthesis, and evaluation. Taken collectively, these intellectual skills can be seen as the anatomy of cognitive learning. A shorthand version of Bloom's taxonomy offers a quick and easy guide to how learning contracts can be organized or designed in respect to those skills.

Knowledge

Bloom divides knowledge into specifics, ways and means, and universals and abstractions. Knowledge of specifics includes (1) terms and symbols: defining terms via attributes, properties, or relations; knowing vocabulary and reading and conversing intelligently; (2) facts: knowing dates, places, names, etc. Ways and

Means includes (1) ways of organizing, studying, judging, and criticizing ideas and phenomena (process): using methods of inquiry; knowing standards of judgment; using techniques and classifications as links between and among facts; (2) conventions: knowing characteristic ways of treating ideas; knowing the use, style, and practice of conventions; knowing form and usage, as in writing; (3) trends and sequences: knowing interrelationships; knowing continuity and development; knowing evolution; (4) classifications and categories: knowing classes, sets, divisions, forms, and types; (5) criteria for judgments; (6) techniques, procedures, and methods. Universals and abstractions include: (1) schemes, patterns, and theories; (2) principles and generalizations; (3) theories, structures, and interrelations.

At Empire State, the student's knowledge is indicated when questions such as these are answered: How much factual information does the student already possess? Does the difficulty level of the contract build on what the student already knows? Does the contract explicitly call for learning new information? Do readings expose the student to the ways in which bodies of knowledge are organized? What guides are available to help the student improve his ability to handle knowledge in characteristic form, style, and usage? Does the contract ask the student to demonstrate these skills? Do the readings provide historical overview or exposure to trends in, continuity in, and expansion of bodies of knowledge, as well as to current models and techniques? Is the student appropriately exposed to major theories held by leading exponents within an area of knowledge? Small segments of actual learning contracts illustrate ways in which students at Empire State are expected by mentors to demonstrate various types of knowledge. In presenting small segments, it must be recognized that both cognitive skills and learning contracts have complex functions, and an isolated segment about specific skills is not necessarily the mark of an outstanding learning contract, and also that any complex learning activity may call for several levels of intellectual competence beyond the retention of information. Therefore, some examples offered here also contain elements of more complex intellectual skills.

EXAMPLES:

"During the course of this contract, the student will be engaged in exploring a number of 'Third Force,' or humanistic, psychologies. The purpose of these studies is to provide the student with a framework and an understanding of the theoretical concepts and objectives of the field of humanistic psychology."

"This contract will be primarily directed toward reading in the field of child development. The purpose of this study is to provide the student with an overview of various theoretical approaches to the emotional and cognitive development of the child, including an exploration of the role of mother-child interaction in personality development. More specifically, this learning program will cover the intellectual, emotional, and social growth of the neonate, infant, toddler, preschool, and school-age child."

"The introductory exploration of theater begun by the student in her previous contract will be extended to a more advanced level through an examination of the theatrical theories of Constantin Stanislavski, Bertolt Brecht, and Jerzy Grotowski. An examination of this kind will provide her with exposure to a wide range of production theories since the three principals—when considered together—embrace most of the theories of theater developed in the centuries of theater history. An extension of this primary focus will be a closer study of the work of Brecht. Again, her initial readings will provide a general familiarity of the work of the three theater artists which will be amplified as the contract progresses."

"The student will familiarize herself with a wide array of textbooks in the field of child psychology and development in order to obtain an appreciation of different approaches and points of view regarding child development. Two of the more popular texts are by Stone and Church and by Mussen, Conger and Kagan. She should include in her readings works on personality, e.g., Hall and Lindsay, and in cognitive development, e.g., Elkind and Piaget."

Comprehension

In the area of comprehension, Bloom included (1) translation from one level of abstraction to another, from one symbolic form to another, from one verbal form to another; (2) interpretation to reorder or arrange, to avoid "reading in" one's own ideas, to recognize limits within which interpretations can be drawn, to distinguish between warranted and unwarranted conclusions; (3) extrapolation to project consequences and ramifications, to extend trends beyond the data, to infer with some degree of probability, to conclude, to predict, to estimate.

Learning contract questions at Empire State regarding comprehension include these: Is the student asked to translate from the abstract to the concrete? To interpret and give meaning to isolated situations? To translate complex communications into simpler forms? To state a situation "in his own words"? To illustrate, or to give examples? Is the student given clear opportunities to attempt his own interpretations? Are there sufficient avenues of "feedback", trial and error, and other interactions with the mentor or other more experienced scholars? Can a student recycle his efforts so that he can learn through experience about his own interpretative limits? To what extent do the learning activities require the student to extend, to infer, and to conclude? Does the learning contract include a systematic element with which the student must deal? Is the student asked to assess the "givens" in a situation and to make and project inferences?

Examples from actual learning contracts illustrate various forms of comprehension.

EXAMPLES:

"The student will choose four pairs of buildings from the following periods/places: Egypt and the Near East; Greece and Rome; Early Christian; Medieval; Renaissance; Baroque; Nineteenth Century; Twentieth Century. The purpose of this will be to do a comparative analysis of the buildings which will reveal some of the extra-architectural considerations that may have influenced the designs in some way. The comparisons will be presented in the form of detailed lessons with the appropriate visual materials included."

"Using available bibliographic materials, the student will write a research paper on the Virology of Human Tumors. The scope of the paper should be that of a scientific review article, and should be designed to show the following:

1. The student's comprehension of basic biological and chemical processes.
2. Clarity of exposition.
3. Evidence of the student's ability to grasp the methodology of biomedical research.
4. Evidence of the student's ability to distinguish between proofs, working hypotheses, and conjectures.
5. Evidence of the student's capacity to understand the limitations as well as the promise of any given area of investigation."

"After having read *Manchild in the Promised Land,* the student will define what she perceived to be Claude Brown's basic view of his world and the value system which seems to have produced this view. She will apply this definition to her own life or the lives of the population with whom she is working, explaining why the book has given her a better understanding of a culture."

Application

Bloom includes here the use of abstractions in particular and concrete situations and the remembering and applying of principles, ideas, and theories. Learning contract questions include: Does the learning contract ask the student, in a variety of ways, to apply theories to his own real-life experience? Are field work projects linked to the study of theory? Does the learning contract give the student practical problems to solve, and the relevant work to be done?

Learning contract examples of application include these:

EXAMPLES:

"The student will tape a series of singing lessons. First he will make a tape of a lesson where he begins to work with a student on the interpretation of a song. Then he will listen to the tape, write a summary and critical analysis, and make a written plan for the next lesson. He will then tape the next lesson, listen to it, make a transcript, summary and critical analysis, and plan the next lesson."

"The student will be doing field research in the Azores, living and working in one or two small villages. The Purposes will be to: (1) study women of the Azores by living and working among them; (2) observe and participate in religious practices and economic exchanges; (3) determine the effect that the economy and religious beliefs play in the role of a woman; (4) determine the women's duties in child rearing; and (5) understand how religion and economic factors interrelate in women's overall roles and duties."

"Weisman and Aron describe research techniques in connection with field work projects. The student will become knowledgeable about these techniques and will select three she feels would be most valuable as tools for research carried on by her department. She will then undertake three small research projects."

"As a part of this contract, the student will develop a rationale for motel siting on Lake George and other major Adirondack Lakes. This must take into consideration the aesthetic, economic and environmental factors related to such land-use planning. A map will be prepared showing the present location and size of motels on Lake George as a starting point. This map will be redrawn with overlays to indicate other configurations which would take into consideration the above mentioned factors. Zoning, sign control, cluster housing, condominiums, camping, etc., must be included as they apply to the motel siting. The student will also study the reports of the Lake Champlain-Lake George Regional Planning Board as they apply to this project."

Analysis

Bloom classifies here the ability to identify elements, to recognize unstated assumptions, to distinguish facts from hypotheses, to identify connections and interactions between elements and parts, to check consistency of hypotheses with given information, to comprehend interrelationships among ideas, to perceive the organization, systematic arrangement, and structure which hold a communication together, to recognize form and pattern, and to recognize general techniques. Learning contract questions at this level include: Do the learning activities ask the student to acquire new analytical skills? Is the student exposed to new readings and experiences which must be identified by their elements, by their connections, by their form and pattern? Is the student asked to demonstrate his ability to recognize discrete elements, relationships, and large-scale organizational principles?

Segments of learning contracts that illustrate analysis include these:

EXAMPLES:

"A comparative analysis of the Montessori School and the student's own teaching will be made, emphasizing effectiveness and responsiveness of the child. References will be cited in the analysis."

"The student's purpose in this contract is to develop analytical skills in reading. At the same time, the student will be investigating the historical development of the novel in English Literature. Both of these matters relate directly to her creative writing, which is at the center of this contract. She needs to read to learn specific writing techniques, and she needs to know how those techniques developed through time, where things stand today, and possible directions in the future. In addition to her participation in the creative writing seminar, the student will write an analytical paper on the development of the novel and will write four original pieces of material, either fiction or poetry."

"The student will do two papers which will attempt to tie together her readings in this contract with her past work in American History and with the readings that she did on American art in her last contract. These papers will deal with the relationships of art (literary and visual) to the idea of nature and to the process of industrialization in 19th century America."

"After reading The Scarlet Letter, Moby Dick, and The Crucible, the student is to deal with the following questions:

1. How do these books characterize Puritan society?
2. How does this characterization relate to the author's broader historical perception?
3. Who are Hester Prynne, Dimmsdale, Chillingsworth, Pearl in terms of the phenomena, tendencies, etc., that they represent?
4. Ditto for Captain Ahab, and why does he curse the sun?
5. Ditto for witch trials?
6. How do these works approach the "question of women"?
7. How do these books wrench the "Puritan Dilemma" out of the seventeenth century? Do they?
8. Do you think this wrenching is justified?"

Synthesis

Bloom here covers the ability to develop a communication that conveys ideas, feelings, and/or experiences to organize ideas to develop a plan of work or propose a plan of operation or outline of requirements, to develop sets of abstract relations to classify or explain data or to deduce relationships from sets of basic propositions, to formulate appropriate hypotheses, and to modify hypotheses in light of new factors. Learning contract questions here might be: Is the student asked to coordinate diverse information into a meaningful and cohesive unit? To integrate diverse reactions and experiences orally or in writing? To synthesize data collected by him or by others? Does the contract call for a plan of action to be developed?

Two segments of actual contracts illustrate synthesis:

EXAMPLES:

"The activities related to the seminar on the Teaching of Reading, assisting the reading teacher, and the bibliography, will be synthesized in a program development for the teaching of reading. This program will be presented to the seminar group and will be additionally developed in written form."

"The student will keep a journal of her reactions and impressions to each of the dance, art, music, and theater events included in the contract, and will culminate the entire experience with an extensive paper on the subject: The Flux of Response. The paper will deal with her reactions to the events she will have attended and will try to get at the nature of her responses to art—the differences and similarities of response to differing art forms and to different events of the same art form."

"At the conclusion of her reading the works in each bibliography indicated, the student will write two papers on the following:

1. An analysis of the questions and new problem areas which the readings pose for her. She will describe these reactions in written projects and will include how these areas might be pursued in future study.
2. An analysis of how the readings have either changed or reinforced her conceptions and beliefs about sociology in general; about the nature, extent and cause of social problems; and about the nature, extent and structure of human service systems."

Evaluation

Bloom identifies here the ability to make judgements about the value of materials and methods, to make quantitative and qualitative judgements about the satisfaction of criteria and use of standards of appraisal; to evaluate a communication from evidence of logical accuracy, consistency, exactitude, documentation, proof, etc., and to evaluate material by selected or remembered criteria in the field, as with other material of recognized excellence. Questions about learning contracts could include: Is the student asked to make judgements about the work of others or about his own work? Does he have a planned opportunity to see and hear other ideas, and to challenge and interact with those ideas? Is he encouraged to play the Devil's Advocate? Is he asked to help evaluate his own learning contract? Is he asked to distinguish fact from emotion, to identify evidence and weight it?

These examples from contracts illustrate evaluation.

EXAMPLES:

"The goal is to study some of the prevalent theories and techniques used in the treatment of emotionally ill persons. To point out some of the contrasting treatments and to compare and comment on what, in the student's opinion, are valid concepts for good treatment and what may cause further trauma through stigmatizing, labeling or patterning by what are now acceptable methods. The student will read books, both prose and poetry, concerning theories of treatment, the personal experiences, and the institutional and societal ways of dealing with the disfigured and emotionally disturbed, and other types of social deviants."

"This contract deals with the question of pollution and pollution control of the Chenango River, and includes a project consisting of the following activities:

1. Define pollution.
2. Summarize existing laws pertaining to the pollution and pollution control of the Chenango River.
3. Summarize data of analysis done on the Chenango River for the past five years.
4. Report on the measures being taken by industries along the Chenango River to reduce emissions into the river.
5. Report on the natural pollutants of the Chenango River.
6. Correlate the relationship of legislation to pollution and pollution control.
7. Look into the possible effects of river quality on the populace adjacent to the river.
8. Obtain a public profile on the Chenango River quality.
9. Make a judgement as to the improvement or deterioration of conditions and suggest future action."

"The Farmer's Museum in Cooperstown, New York, and Old Sturbridge Village in Sturbridge, Mass., are two of many examples of 'museums without walls' to be found throughout the country. One of their common objectives is to preserve the flavor and texture of life in our country at an earlier time through a study of the crafts. The student is to prepare a written defense of the concept that the crafts serve as a valid means of interpreting a given culture to persons of another age."

In summary, the above examples illustrate efforts made by the mentors and students working together to identify and define learning experiences that will foster intellectual skills, areas of *compre-*

hension, application, analysis, synthesis, and *evaluation,* the major parts of the taxonomy of cognitive learning developed by Bloom and others.

ASSESSING LEARNING CONTRACTS

One of the problems with most innovative programs in higher education is the lack of significant attempts to assess the learning experiences of the students. While it should be recognized that the Empire State College program does not have a lengthy period of service for such evaluation, there is some information available which suggests some of the strengths and weaknesses of this approach to learning.

A 1974 survey of over 250 Empire State students indicated that 46 percent evaluated the learning contract as superior to traditional learning methods, 26 percent rated it "somewhat better," 13 percent considered it "comparable," and only 2 percent deemed it "somewhat inferior." When students were asked about the learning contract's contribution to personal development, 58 percent checked "much more valuable than regular college course," 12 percent checked "a little more valuable," and 12 percent "about the same." More specifically, 86 percent of the students indicated that they were interested by, and attracted to, the work their contracts called for, 76 percent said that they were challenged and that learning resources were available when they needed them, and 71 percent indicated that they felt confident and competent in relation to the work they were doing. Approximately 65 percent found that they were being stimulated and that new worlds were "opening up." A minority of students reported negative feelings about contracts. Thirteen percent were worried about evaluation, 4 percent were confused and unclear, and 3 percent were bored and uninterested.

Learning contracts pose challenges for evaluation, and the questionnaire addressed this problem. When evaluation was done directly by the mentor it was generally satisfactory—61 percent yes, 8 percent no, 20 percent uncertain, 10 percent no response. When done by others it was judged less satisfactory. One evaluative component of many contracts is a log or journal kept by the student. An item analysis of the logs indicates that 35 percent of the students who kept logs used them to record reflections on readings, reactions, thoughts relevant to their daily lives, trying to put their contract activities in a larger context of their past experience and the present circumstances. Seventeen percent indicated that the log was basically a record of contract activities, and another 17 percent described it as a history of their record at Empire State.

When students were asked to list the major weaknesses in the learning contract methods, the largest group, 24 percent, wrote "no weaknesses." Significant proportions called attention to several major problem areas. Fifteen percent were bothered by the lack of group exchange. Ten percent mentioned the need for self-discipline. Eight percent felt that they were too dependent on one mentor. Smaller proportions found it difficult to allocate their time well, needed more structure, found contracts difficult to write and resources hard to find, felt they could not explore interests beyond the contract, and that the Empire State program was confused or confusing.

Despite the independent and sometimes lonely nature of Empire State College studies, 33 percent of the students reported some involvement in group studies or workshops. Learning contracts for field or work experiences were used by 57 percent of the responding students. Tutors were used for specialized knowledge and professional advice, and adjunct faculty were used by 19 percent of the students. Among other learning resources, print predominated, with 73 of the 250 students mentioning libraries, and 52 noting books and periodicals. Courses at other colleges were used by 34 students and considerable diversity was shown in the use of professionals from museums and galleries, community organizations, government, the mass media, and education.

Empire State College learning contracts appear to call for higher order cognitive processes "almost all the time" or a "great deal." Seventy-four percent of the responding students checked one of these categories for Synthesis; Evaluation by 61 percent, Application by 60 percent, and 70 percent for Analysis. Memorizing either a great deal or almost all the time was reported by only 15 percent of the students; 41 percent said they spent "very little time" memorizing. On a four-point scale, the modal response in all locations was the second highest point ("a great deal") for Analysis, Synthesis, and Evaluation. Forty-seven percent of the students reported that the college was a major influence in regard to increasing intellectual competence and curiosity. Thirty-five percent also reported increasing job related competence. At the other end of the scale, three percent and nineteen percent respectively indicated that these two cognitive abilities were not increased at all. More than 30 percent said that they were influenced "to a major extent" in regard to affective abilities of self-reliance, self-understanding, and awareness. From 16 percent to 26 percent reported influence to a major extent in clarifying purposes, self-consistency, understanding others, and interpersonal competence. Students indicating moderate influence by the College ranged from 28 percent to 35 percent in all of these affective categories, while those reporting no influence ranged from 9 percent in awareness to 18 percent in interpersonal competence.

In general, then, Empire State College students encounter a situation generally perceived as being less formal, less structured and less "traditional" than most institutions of higher learning. In contrast, students who characterize themselves as having clear and certain learning objectives and who do not radically depart from them have overwhelmingly positive experiences in the Empire State environment. Specifically, such students view themselves as actively involved in the learning process through the contract method and feel able to pursue their individual goals. These students indicate a high degree of satisfaction with the Empire State College program, with outcomes in both the affective and cognitive domain. As a direct consequence of the mentoring process, almost half of the respondents perceive themselves engaged in a process superior to that characterized as traditional. In short, these students perceive Empire State College and the use of the contract learning approach as an important and necessary vehicle in that it provides the opportunity to engage in interesting, challenging and stimulating learning. For this group Empire State College is perceived as helping to develop confidence and competence by fostering self-reliance, self-understanding, clarifying purposes, self-consistency, understanding others and a sense of interpersonal skill. In addition, students express satisfaction with both the process and the outcome of assuming decision-making responsibility regarding the development of their learning contracts.

6 ARGENTINE S. CRAIG

Contracting in a University Without Walls Program

It has become increasingly clear that any major changes to established academic patterns require that reform movements strike out independently to create alternative models rather than attempting to integrate into existing ones.

University Without Walls at Morgan State College is part of such a reform movement on a national level.* Basically, the University Without Walls is an alternative plan for undergraduate education that can lead to a degree. It is called the University Without Walls because " . . . it abandons the tradition of a sharply circumscribed campus and provides education for students wherever they may be—at work, in their homes, in prisons, through internships, independent study and field experiences, within areas of special social problems, at one or more colleges and in travel and service abroad. It abandons the traditional classroom as the principal instrument of instruction, as well as the prescribed curriculum, the grades and credit points. It enlarges the faculty to include knowledgeable people from outside the academic world and makes use of modern educational technology for storage, retrieval and communication of knowledge . . . " (University Without Walls, 1971). It places strong emphasis on student self-

*University Without Walls is a program of the Union for Experimenting Colleges and Universities (UECU), an association of 29 institutions that have joined to encourage research and experimentation in higher education.

direction while still recognizing and providing for the special needs of the educationally disadvantaged. It stresses the importance of maintaining close teaching-learning relations between student, teachers and others. It aims to create an attitude of life-long learning.

This non-traditional educational model has been recognized internationally as a viable alternative for undergraduate education. Nationally, there are 30* colleges and universities developing UWW units and enrolling over 3000 students in the bachelor's program and approximately 300 in the UECU's Ph.D. program. Institutions outside of the United States have begun initiating the development of UWW centers. A UNESCO grant of $10,000 and a grant from the Ford Foundation have provided the UECU an opportunity to arrange conferences abroad involving educators from the European and Third World countries in 1972 and 1973.

UWW at Morgan State University actually began when King V. Cheek brought the idea with him to Morgan State in 1971 when he became president. He states: "We began with a few assumptions: that higher education had to develop some alternative modes of education different from the typical rigid classroom structure; that higher education should be available to students from 16 to 60 no matter where they are. We had these reasons: First cost; the cost of higher education is becoming very expensive, especially in the area of capital outlays and faculty costs. And it became clear in the '60s and is clear now, that there is tremendous dissatisfaction on the part of students and faculty with the way we are educating our students. We are also directing this concept at continuing education so learning will be available to all ages. The UWW porgram provides another alternative in education, which

*University of Alabama (New College), Antioch College, Bard College, Universidad Boricua, Chicago State University, College of Racine, Florida International University, Franconia College, Friends World College, Goddard College, Hofstra University, Howard University, Johnston College, Kirkland College, Loretto Heights College, University of Massachusetts, University of Minnesota, Morgan State College, Northeastern Illinois University, University of the Pacific, Pitzer College, Roger Williams College, Shaw University, Skidmore College, University of South Carolina, Staten Island Community College, Stephens, Webster College, Westminster College, University of Wisconsin at Green Bay.

should have multiple alternatives because we have a heterogeneous population, and education should be responsive." Although Morgan State's UWW seeks out those who have been traditionally under-represented in higher education—Blacks and other minorities, women, prisoners, veterans, the older student—the program operates on an open admissions policy, admitting students who want to learn using the UWW approach. The focus is on new approaches to teaching and learning via learning contracts and implementing equal educational opportunities because tradition and race have been and continue to be two of the major barriers to higher education. Since 1971, approximately 250 students have been admitted to UWW at Morgan. Of this number more than 50% are women, 75% minorities, 70% over thirty, 15% veterans, and 5% prison inmates. More than 50% are considered economically "disadvantaged." The program stresses competency, based on achievement of learning objectives and performance criteria, individually defined. Individualization of the education process is the core of the total UWW program, conducted in the learning environment of the home, the college, the world of work and using the total resources of the wider community made available through a range of educational technology.

The program is unique in its attempt to determine readiness for a degree without counting the hours spent in the classroom or the numerical average of grades received in courses but rather through a series of completed learning contracts that are reviewed during three evaluation sessions. Designed with the goal of building a new framework designed around a set of alternative basic concepts (UWW: *First Report,* February, 1972), the process begins at the point of admission with an assessment of the student's document of prior learning experiences.* Through it the student communicates what it is she has learned and how it is related to her goals. The program's staff assists the student in identifying relevant learning, documenting it in a way that is easily communicated to others. Staff members with adjunct advisors and outside examiners

---

*The document of prior learning experiences is a five page form that asks questions dealing with employment (job titles and descriptions, skills learned); other experiences relevant to educational objectives (college courses, workshops, conferences, travel); growth.

assess the learning experiences presented in the document. It is at this point that a student begins to negotiate her educational experiences based on her value system. As she engages in this process, clarification of goals and concepts of what is worth knowing evolve.

It is at those assessment sessions that questions are raised (for consideration, not necessarily for answers), regarding goals and objectives: Is your goal to know . . . understand . . . appreciate . . . enjoy . . . believe . . . have faith in . . . , is it to write . . . to recite . . . to identify . . . to differentiate . . . to solve . . . to construct . . . to compare . . . to contrast? Since objectives can best be stated in question form, the student is asked: What are the questions for which *you* are seeking answers? What do you need and want to learn? If the student's decision is to acquire, in an independent way, a well-rounded liberal arts background before delving deeply into a particular field, options are offered that look something like this:

Traditional Requirements in General Education	Options for Acquiring General Knowledge via UWW Learning Contracts
50 credits in general education (English Composition, Social Sciences, Humanities, Natural Sciences, Health and Physical Education)	A. Independent study resulting in performance competencies demonstrated by the passing of proficiency examinations or the CLEP tests of the College Boards. and/or B. Interdisciplinary Seminar (Participation in weekly three hour seminar for a 12-24 month period) and/or C. Assessment of knowledge acquired through life experiences.
50 credits in general education:	D. Development areas (the following can also demonstrate competency and academic scholarship):
(1) English	(1) Journal (maintenance of a daily journal throughout enrollment in program) and Written self-evaluations for all contracted learning experiences, and Projects, internships with newspapers

Traditional Requirements in General Education	Options for Acquiring General Knowledge via UWW Learning Contracts
	or magazines, written work related to overall Developmental Plan.
(2) Social Sciences	(2) Independent Study (Directed readings in the fields of sociology, psychology, anthropology, political science and education, and/or Educational Television courses in the field of social sciences and/or Internships (See UWW Directory of Learning Resources)
(3) Humanities	(3) Independent Study (Directed readings in the field of Humanities and/or Educational Courses: Drama Seminars in the Arts and/or Travel/ Study Projects (home or abroad to study other cultures and life styles)
(4) Sciences: Natural, Physical, Biological	(4) (The rationale and objectives for the traditional science requirements are interpreted by UWW to be for: (a) the development of an understanding of scientific inquiry and critical thought, and (b) the integration and application of scientific principles to solve societal problems.) Suggest: Scientific Projects in ecology, drugs, nutrition, hypertension. Written Reports (review of the literature, writing abstract of scientific studies of society). Work experience or internships with agencies involved in scientific work. Educational Television Courses: The Study of Biology, Environment, Astronomy. Spectrum series (field studies that are now under the auspices of leading world scientists

from a Moscow operating room to a physics laboratory at Johns Hopkins University). Laboratory experiments (portable minilab from the Open University).

(5) Health and Physical Education

(5) Participation and membership in a health/physical education activity with the Y's, Scouts, Little League neighborhood recreational groups. Informal recreational activities with family, friends, neighbors (bicycling, jogging, tennis, golf, swimming, etc.). Personal health program for physical fitness and athletic skills.

At a later time, during another session, this information on the student's prior learning experiences becomes useful in helping to determine and outline future projects. At the end of the assessment negotiation, an agreement is made on what experiences are relevant to present goals, although no credits, advance standing or grades are assigned. The past learning experiences are acknowledged; demonstrated competencies are summarized and entered on the transcript in narrative form. The purpose of the goal development process is that recognition is given to the varied personal, community and job-related experiences that people bring with them when they enter the program. Psychologically, the good that is done for a person's self-esteem is important in many ways. Experiences heretofore thought to have no "educational" or academic value, when viewed in the context of goals, become parts of a continuum of learning experiences that may contribute an overall plan:

A DEVELOPMENTAL PLAN has been designed and approved for:

(Student's Name)
_____

DEVELOPMENTAL GOAL:

Ms. R. is interested in developing her career within the nursing/ sociology area, with focus on family counseling. She will be working toward her Bachelor of Science degree through the Union for Experimenting College and Universities. In conjunction with Ms. R's efforts in career development and her educational pursuits, the following program has been outlined to assist her in achieving these goals.

DEVELOPMENTAL PLAN (Steps to pursue goal in next 12 mos.)

Areas of Study:

Sociology, Nursing Practitioner (work experience at clinic), Urban Problems in Housing, Family Counseling.

Special Projects:

Community volunteer work (problems in social areas such as drugs, juvenile delinquency).

Development of film library (annotated) on family counseling.

Courses Recommended:

See attached list; note courses with asterisk(*)

Readings Recommended:

General work-related readings: Medicare and the Hospital (Somers); Interpersonal Dynamics (Bennis, Schein, Steele), Family Therapy (Acherman).

Specialized readings (to be recommended by adjuncts).

UWW Student

UWW Director

UWW Program Advisor

Date approved: _____

Helping a student to develop her goals and create learning contracts to reach those goals takes many hours of staff and adjunct advisors' time. In terms of costs, there are many financial factors related to student goal development, enrollment and staffing. For example, before a student's assessment session, she has been given a personal interview of approximately two hours, during which time she is encouraged to express through writing her past experiences that are relevant to her present goals. The assessment session itself usually takes two hours and involves at least three persons. Conferences of one to two hours are scheduled to create contracts for desired experiences. If a student is interested in developing six contracts per year, the time involved could be four to six hours. Since the contract usually is between the student and a person other than a UWW staff person, additional conference time between the student and the adjunct advisors should be considered. Students meet with their advisors on the average of twice a month for at least one hour per meeting. Adjunct advisors are usually paid $5.00 per hour; outside examiners, $10 per hour; and program advisors (staff) earn approximately $6.00 per hour. Advising costs (in gross figures) amount to approximately $636 per student per year, based on:

2 hour personal interview (advisor, $12; staff $12; volunteer)	$ 24
2 hour assessment session (advisor, $12; adjunct, $10; examiner $20)	42
6 contract conferences @ $6 (UWW program advisor)	36
6 contract conferences @ $5 (adjunct advisor)	30
24 individual conferences among three adjunct advisors (72 @ $5 p.h.)	360
24 individual conferences with program advisor	144
	$636

The above model is an "external" type that is workable for the student who does not use any college facilities or resources (regular classes), but instead is studying independently with the help of advisors and using the resources of the city. Income realized would be $159,000 (250x$636); advising costs would amount to $150,000.

Expenses can also be kept at a minimum in the model that utilizes college facilities and resources. For example, if a program advisor spends approximately 36 hours (interview, assessment, individual conference) with each student, having 1920 hours (40x48) available for that period, she would be able to advise approximately 50 students. The program would need five full-time program advisors at a total cost of $60,000. If a student has three contracts and relates to three adjunct advisors during the year, the program would need 750 adjunct advisors. If each met with her student two hours per month and was paid $5.00 per hour, it would cost the program $90,000 for adjunct advisors' services. The total advising cost to the program would amount to $150,000.

In addition, there are the vitally needed services of secretaries, clericals and administrators to handle and process the written evaluations, contracts, the paper work attendant to narrative transcripts and other personalized services characteristic of a non-traditional program that must be coordinated. These non-instructional personnel positions would require approximately $40,000. Add $5,000 more for office supplies, materials, equipment; $16,000 (8% for overhead) to provide for office and conference space, utilities, janitorial services. The expenses are now approaching the $200,000 mark, which may not be prohibitive in light of overall program operation with the outcomes of a quality program based on learning contracts.

The fact of the matter is the contract model as described may cost no more to operate than the traditional educational program. With the aim of developing a self-supporting program, the cost to the student (at UWW/Morgan State) for fiscal year 1974 is only $824.50 for a 12 month learning program ($325.50 per semester and $173.50 for the summer session), yielding an income of approximately $206,000 ($824.50x250 full time students), which is adequate to meet the expenses as outlined. In practice, University Without Walls at Morgan State has an operating budget for fiscal 1974 of over $200,000 with $118,000 coming from federal sources and the remainder from UWW student tuition and fees. The low cost to the student is consistent with the philosophy of offering educational opportunity to a wider constituency. Such a low cost is possible because of the volunteer services of many adjunct advisors. These are community people, heads of departments in industry, M.D.'s at hospitals, Ph.D's at other institutions, supervisors at work stations, teachers in the public and private school systems, newspaper editors, artists, musicians, the Morgan State College faculty and so forth. In short, an incalculable contribution is made in terms of human resources. Additionally, the college provides some facilities and services (space, electricity, heat, accounting reports) out of the 8% indirect costs from the federal grants. Moreover, students can register for and attend regular courses offered by the college and other state colleges at no additional charge beyond their payment of full-time tuition/fees. These are the practical realities of the financial factors which require creative use of existing resources to support innovation. Contract learning at Morgan State is not only a financially viable model, but is academically effective. There is agreement on the point among many individuals in higher education that it is no longer practical (or even desirable) to standardize courses of study. Moreover, the circumstances and settings into which students go are too diverse to prescribe a curriculum that would suit all.

The learning contract is a way to individualize learning so that the learner can create and organize her own curriculum. The contract is considered a clearly defined agreement between responsible individuals. Its value lies in the freedom it affords the student in drawing up the terms and negotiating her education on those terms. She is able to bring together resources not brought together before, thus creating a unique situation for herself. The learning contract represents something approaching equality of power between her and the teacher (learning facilitator). For each learning experience, including regular courses, a learning contract is developed that specifies the experience to be acquired and carries a commitment of written evaluations by the student and her adjunct advisor. The student also documents all of her learning experiences in a journal, which serves as another evaluative tool.

Most of the UWW units use some sort of learning contract because it has been found to be an effective educational instrument consistent with the UWW philosophy and objectives. The contract presently used at UWW/Morgan State was adopted in February, 1973. Questions raised are: What specific behaviors will you be able to demonstrate as a result of this experience? What content, topics, specific sub-areas of interest will you explore during this experience? What learning strategies will you use to achieve the stated objectives? How do you know when you have mastered your objectives? What texts and collateral readings will you use?

For the most part, students are excited and serious about their contracts. A letter from one student stated:

After many months of uncertainty, I am happy to announce

that my request for sabbatical leave from the Department of Health, Education and Welfare has been approved, and I will be devoting full time to my studies in the University Without Walls at Morgan. I plan to complete my formal coursework and final project by June, 1974. Two of the learning contracts which were made in February for courses in Psychology and Statistics have been completed. Evaluations of my experiences and a copy of the transcripts of grades in these courses are attached. I underestimated the time and difficulties involved in the third contract I made to study the career and upward mobility program I have administered here at HEW since June 1971. I have revised the title of this contract to "Changes in the System—An Evaluation of an Internal DHEW Career Development and Upward Mobility Program" and I plan to use this for my final project. Please attach the revised face page to the contract previously submitted. My adjunct advisor's data sheet and personal resume are also included in the attachments to this letter. I am planning to request advisors from the psychology department at Morgan, however, I have not approached anyone as yet. I do realize that time is passing very swiftly and my program advisor has encouraged me . . .

One of the contracts referred to in the letter from the student was Psychological Statistics which she developed in this order: What specific behaviors will you be able to demonstrate as a result of this experience and under what situations?

"To collect, organize, analyze and summarize data on my job when preparing reports and statistical tables on the training activities of 250 people in HEW."

What content, topics, specific sub-areas of interests will you explore during this experience?

1. Frequency distributions
2. Percentile ranks
3. Measures of central tendency
4. Measures of dispersion
5. Normal distribution
6. Standard scores
7. Research methods
8. Pearson Product Moment Correlation
9. Biserial correlation
10. Spearman correlation
11. Phi correlation
12. Tetrachordic correlation
13. Sampling theory
14. T-Test for Related samples
15. T-Test for independent samples
16. Chi-square test of independence

What learning strategies will you use to achieve the objectives stated?

"Develop schedule for homework. Seek counseling from instructor. Seek tutoring from statistician."

How do you know when you have mastered your objectives?

"I will be able to identify appropriate methods for preparing reports and statistical tables."

What texts and collateral readings will you use?

"Fundamental Research Statistics by John T. Roscoe."

The contract was a four-month one and, at the end of the contracted time, the student had this to say about the learning experience:

> I elected to take this course because I felt that it would help me in my job of preparing reports and statistical tables on the training activities of 250 people in HEW. I needed to be sure I was selecting the appropriate method of data collection and to prepare this information so that it could be easily interpreted by high officials in the organization. I have learned from this course that statistical data on the career progression of employees must be of a sophistication that will sell the program. I have learned to identify the appropriate methods for preparing reports and statistical tables by going through many exercises with the methods listed. When I started this course I had to develop a personal time schedule for adequate time to devote to the homework exercises. I also felt a knowledge gap in algebra and geometry which I had taken more than 17 years ago. Nevertheless, I was determined to overcome this gap by going to the instructor for coaching during his free periods and getting further tutoring from a senior statistician on the job. When difficulties arose concerning the terminology, I decided to take my cassette tape recorder to class and tape the lectures so that I could replay the lesson on the way home from work and while traveling to school. This technique worked wonders for me, as I was able to synthesize this highly technical information . . . . I have mastered the subject by the learning techniques mentioned and am able to select the best method for preparing reports."

Other evaluations than those of student statements are used in the Morgan State program. In a memo to a program advisor another student wrote:

The following is intended as a briefing as of June, 1973 regarding my learning contracts with UWW and progress as of that date. As of the above date, I consider two objectives in the original contracts completed. They are the courses pursued at Johns Hopkins University: Principles of Sociology and Electronic Data Processing. The transcript . . . indicates that both were completed satisfactorily. I have diligently attempted to keep a daily and/or periodic log concerning the other contracts which are detailed below:

1. URBAN AFFAIRS.

I have endeavored to apply a variety of learning experiences to the fulfillment of what I consider a most important area. Paramount among these experiences has been a daily contact with my adjunct advisor, Jerome Monaghan. . . . has been invaluable as far as advising me in many aspects of my job. This advice occurs in many forms, such as evaluating my written reports and proposals and offering suggestions as to areas which warrant improvement when appropriate, discussions relating to interpretation of Equal Employment Opportunity legislation and subsequent implementation of such legislation as it affects the work we are doing as the company's E.E.O. representatives. I have been encouraged by him to initiate proposals for company involvement in community programs not previously undertaken which would clearly indicate a sincere effort to prepare females and minorities for growing opportunities in the world of work, with positive efforts being made to improve existing recruitment channels and to discover new sources of recruitment of the above groups.

One of the major projects which I have initiated has been the establishment of a job awareness program with Dunbar Senior High School . . . a first for the company and hopefully, this will be expanded to include other inner city schools in the future. It is my opinion that the above is a good illustration of what Urban Affairs can and should be, with the Black community deriving the benefits.

Various seminars sponsored by such organizations as the

Chamber of Commerce, American Gas Association and the Baltimore Community Relations Commission have been another mode of my learning experience. Most of these have been related to E.E.O. matters and afforded me the opportunity to hear people from government, man-power agencies and private business who are experts in this particular area. I have also served on various committees of the Morgan and Bowie College Cluster programs, as well as programs sponsored by the National Alliance of Businessmen. It was my personal responsibility to recruit, screen and hire sixty students for summer jobs with our company under the National Association of Business Program.

The above is not intended to be all inclusive of my activities and learning experiences in the Urban Affairs area, but as an illustration of just some of what I consider the more important aspects of my involvement.

2. ART AND MUSIC.

As of this date, my learning experience in this area has consisted of the reading of two books: *Art Is for Everyone* and *Art and Nature Appreciation*. The readings have been supplemented with a visit to the Peale Museum along with readings of articles concerning music and art in local newspapers. Planned are written reports on texts read and also future visits to museums and musical events.

3. COMMUNITY INVOLVEMENT.

I have obtained as my adjunct advisor in this area, John W. Waters who is president of Morgan's Alumni Association and President of the Personnel Administrators' Association of the Baltimore City Public Schools. He is aware of my past interest in community affairs and my current participation on the Echo House and West End Drug Abuse Boards. It is my intention to continue service on these boards and to render whatever assistance I can in helping these organizations continue as a viable force in the Black community. . . . has agreed to meet with me on a periodic basis to monitor my participation in the above.

The student ends the memo saying: "I realize the preceding constitutes a brief sketch of my learning activities and would be glad to go into more detail if you so request. Thanks for the guidance and help you have given in shaping my learning program." A deeper insight into the active forces operating in the development of the goal-setting process by students, assisted by the UWW program advisors, is provided by some examples of other students' programs based on the learning contract model with some specific information on advisory activities shared through advisors' conference notes:

A student in his early twenties, married and a father, developed a 12 month study program which he felt would help him reach his goal: to become proficient in mathematics. This he expressed in a series of learning contracts, whose objectives were to pass advanced calculus tests, achieve an acceptable score on the Graduate Record Examination in mathematics for purposes of admission to graduate school; write papers on mathematics; learn fundamental principles of mathematics; have a faculty member orally state, "You are good in math," be designated by the mathematics department chairman as an assistant to the teacher in a course in differential equations and to take regular courses in mathematics. About these goals and the interactions which evolved during their setting and pursuit, the advisor noted: "puts himself in a role whereby he will be as proficient in math as anyone else graduating from a college program in mathematics. The student discussed alternative ways of learning math besides course work; discussed course work; discussed feelings about responsibility for his own learning program, his own actions. At the next meeting the student stated that he wanted to change regular course work to independent study and began to develop learning contracts. The student expressed a liking for the standard form of contract and commented that he is beginning to understand the UWW concept. The student reported in his journal the reason for dropping past courses was that instructors did not cover things he was interested in and so he started reading things on his own and gets behind." The Advisor noted that the student "comes across as a student who is very creative and drops courses because he desires to pursue certain interests stimulated by such structured courses, but the course has a structured format and content and so he falls behind. Discussed learning contracts . . . formulating accountability factor for specific objectives."

By the third month, the advisor commented: "taking too much, doing things on a superficial level; has not explored things for paper because has been exploring other areas of interest. Feels he cannot explore math and other interests at same time; recommended that he concentrate on some specific area. Conflict between natural sense of curiosity and obligation to carry out responsibility to math. Student likes to cover things in depth. Suggestion was made that he keep a time log of how much he devotes to other interests. Raised question of what is duty? Time pressure imposed on self is taking fun out of learning. Suggested that he not think in terms of a semester as he takes up things to satisfy his curiosity. Student decided he would not take courses for grades, but would focus on three areas in order to help himself impose self-discipline to accomplish things he set out to do. He realized that last semester he had imposed too many things." Five months after the first conference between the advisor and the student, the advisor noted: " . . . discussed learning program as being broad and specific, the need for general education development. The student decided to sign up for 2-3 courses (because of people teaching them plus area of interest that will be involved). Has changed from independent contract to regular course contract. Discussed characteristics of vacillating and making decisions on incoming data." The following month the advisor observed: "student changed strategy of study plan. Arranged all classes close together so there will be no time to waste in between and will audit four classes and register for two. The student will approach course instructors as adjunct advisors. At this point he is pleased with his accomplishment so far. He is, at this point, a little more organized and is keeping appointments." Other comments and observations: ". . . is sitting in on graduate courses; is thinking of sitting in on course at Towson State. Journal is reflecting attempts to bring learning program together." By the Spring of the year, the advisor wrote: " . . . relates he is dropping quantum mechanics course. We explored his reason for dropping and whether his reason and actions are appropriate at this time or whether his dropping classes is another indication of not being responsible to himself as a person and as a learner.

The student revealed that he has not clarified his values in terms of where real responsibility for learning is. Discussed with student his responsibility to himself in making courses and experiences what he desires them to be instead of conforming; also discussed realistic planning, what he can handle in terms of his learning program and responsibilities as a father and husband. Student stated that he will finish taking the courses and then will concentrate on being responsible and commited to himself during the summer through independent study with adjunct advisor." This he did.

Another student developed a 12 month study program which stipulated an immediate goal as Personnel Manager and a future goal as a lawyer. She developed contracts in the following areas: Community internship with legal aid bureau to obtain experience in helping to relate to people (12 month contract); internship with personnel placement office (6 month contract); regular course work in personnel analysis and personnel management (a one semester contract); workshops (weekends) in personnel management to include sensitivity training (4 times a year); educational television course in management principles for two nights a week (3-month contract). The variety of learning experiences selected is consistent with one of the UWW program objectives ("to provide a wide range of learning resources [field experience, educational technology, tutorial arrangement, independent study, travel] . . . so that students have the opportunity to discover the many ways to learn.") When the advisor made a field visit to the student's internship site, it was learned from the supervisor (an attorney) that the student was serving as a paralegal professional advocating cases. He stated, "She communicates with lawyers on cases, reads up on laws and attends workshops, interviews clients and classifies problems, works on cases preparing for court and keeps up correspondence with clients. The contract developed for this internship is outlined below:

TITLE OF LEARNING EXPERIENCE:

UYA Internship: Legal Aid Bureau.

DATE:

September, 1972 to September, 1973.

OBJECTIVES:

To be able to demonstrate the technique of interviewing and screening clients to determine nature of problem and whether or not a client is eligible for legal aid services.

Content, topics, sub-areas of interest to be explored during the experience: Codes of law governing city of Baltimore and State of Maryland, contents of textbook: *Business Law* by Ronald Anderson; attendance at court hearings to learn that process and, in some cases, attend hearings in the place of an attorney.

Learning strategies: readings, lectures, consultations with the bureau's lawyers, research (collecting data to prepare cases for court).

EVALUATION:

When I can work totally independently at Legal Aid on various cases, from beginning to the court; when evaluations from the attorneys at Legal Aid are good; when I am able to discuss various areas of law intelligently.

This was a valuable learning experience for the student because she was contemplating going to law school and by working on a daily basis with lawyers for an entire year, she was exposed to the laws she was reading about and saw them applied to helping poor people to solve their problems. Advisor noted that student has "great social awareness and involvement in community. Feels accomplishment working with people."

Much information has been collected on the learning contract at UWW/Morgan over the past two years. The 250 students have developed over 1000 contracts. The initial concern was the effectiveness of a contract as a teaching/learning tool. A random sampling of students' contracts as of September, 1972, produced evidence that the contracts are effective, that with experience students become more adept at designing their contracts and in most cases meet the objectives as assessed by themselves and their advisors. For each learning experience the student wrote a descriptive evaluation of her work and determined whether or not she satisfied the goal set at the beginning of the learning experience as outlined in the contract. The student also evaluated the contribution which the adjunct advisor made to her learning.

To formulate an idea of what kinds of behavioral change students were aiming for, data was collected from randomly selected contracts of twenty-five, with the following results:

- percentage of statements denoting overt behaviors that are demonstrable and observable (for example: to be able to verbalize, to be able to compare, to be able to demonstrate) (60%);
- percentage of statements denoting covert feelings, (for example: to be able to understand, to be able to appreciate) (20%);
- percentage of statements denoting *different* learning strategies (for example: internships, educational television, independent study) (90%);
- percentage of students *detailing* different topics and content matter researched or explored (36%);
- percentage of students denoting goal setting and measurable flexibility in mastery of objectives of the contract (for example: to be able to verbalize 5-10 different theories regarding the subject) (60%).

Specifically, the kinds of objectives stated in the sample were cognitive (7), performance (8), consequence (1), affective (6), exploratory (2) and unclear (2). The sample was composed of 13 males and 12 females: 18 Blacks and 7 Whites. Ages ranged between 18 and 44; average age, 30.8. The sample represented such fields of study as Mental Health (2), Business Administration (4), Philosophy (2), Social Sciences (4), Pre-Law (3), Education (3), Biology (1), Criminal Justice (1), Playwriting (1), Photography (1), Engineering (1) and undecided (2).

Effectiveness was measured in terms of whether the student met the objectives she set our for herself (Did she learn what she set out to learn). In 85% of the cases, the objectives were met as evaluated by those supervising the learning experience. It is clear that for UWW/Morgan State, the learning contract is a viable and effective educational instrument, and that the difficulty lies initially in stating and specifying what the objective is and then phrasing it concisely so that it is measurable. Continued use of the learning contract is projected, with data analysis and evaluation as ongoing and integral functions of the program.

7

NEAL R. BERTE

Bringing About Change
in a Traditional Institution
by Learning Contracts

NEW COLLEGE—THE UNIVERSITY OF ALABAMA
CASE STUDY NUMBER ONE

Art Keeney came to New College with a unique situation which needed a unique solution. Art had over thirty years of professional experience in T.V., radio, and newspaper work, but no college degree. He had edited newspapers, scripted national news broadcasts, and was at the time everything in a public relations capacity for a city school board. He wanted an interdisciplinary depth-study in communication-education and desired an undergraduate degree.

If Art had entered any other division of the University he would have begun with only eight hours credit. However, through New College and with the help of the Departments of Broadcast and Film Communication and Journalism, Art was able to receive fifty-nine hours credit for his past experience in broadcasting and print journalism. Art produced cassettes, videotapes, newspapers, awards, letters of recognition and support to prove his competence in the areas covered by the courses. This credit for past experience coupled with College Level Examination Placement (CLEP) credit meant that Art began his college work with seventy semester hours instead of eight.

After his admission to New College Art continued to weave journalism, broadcasting, and education into an interdisciplinary depth-study. Before graduation Art prepared and completed an independent study dealing with psychology and public relations. The study called for Art to produce a public relations campaign for a Half-Way House for Alcoholics. Art produced a twenty minute slide presentation, writing and taping the script and taking over four hundred photographs for use in the presentation. He also designed and edited an entire twelve-page brochure and wrote over fifty radio and television spots for public service use. Art completed the study during the three-week interim term and received academic credit.

Presently Art is working on a masters degree in the Administration of Higher Education after earning his undergraduate degree in two semesters plus a summer on campus.

CASE STUDY NUMBER TWO

Mary Lynn Pike entered New College as a sophomore with an interest in social work, particularly work with youth. By the spring of her junior year this interest had developed into the beginnings of a program in Correctional Psychology. This program preceded the University Program in Correctional Psychology by almost two years.

Her program put together course work from a variety of divisions across the campus. Child and Human Development from the School of Home Economics, Abnormal Psychology, Statistics from Psychology, Criminology from the Sociology Department, Adjudication of Social Issues from the Business Law Department. This combination of courses for an "interdisciplinary depth-study" would have been impossible without New College.

In addition to regular University courses, Mary Lynn designed an independent study through New College entitled "The Disadvantaged Child and His Family." During the project Mary Lynn worked both with the Chief Probation officer at the Juvenile Court and with a faculty member from the Human Development department of the University. She set as her goals a better understanding of the court and the children who pass through it. To meet these goals Mary Lynn met regularly with the probation officer and faculty. In addition, she completed several projects at the court, read books and articles relevant to her study, and kept a journal of her experience. For this project Mary Lynn received three semester hours of credit.

Mary Lynn chose to spend her last semester before graduation in an out-of-class learning project. She designed an experience with the Law Enforcement Academy at The University of Alabama. The Academy includes six weeks of full-time training for police recruits from across the state of Alabama. The training covers the gamut from theories of criminology to marksmanship. Mary Lynn proposed to attend the Academy just as a rookie and afterwards spend two weeks with the Director of the Academy evaluating the past session and planning for the next one. In addition, Mary Lynn read several books, completed a paper, and was evaluated by a professor from the Correctional Psychology department. She received nine semester hours credit for her work with the Law Enforcement Academy. Presently Mary Lynn is attending Graduate School in Correctional Psychology at The University of Alabama.

CASE STUDY NUMBER THREE

Barbara Duke entered New College because she "wanted to become a person." She was already enrolled in the Arts and Sciences division of the University, but felt she might have a more meaningful experience in the New College. Her academic interests were primarily with the Humanities and the Social Sciences.

Barbara eventually put together a depth-study in correctional psychology with a long-range goal of psychology graduate school which was eventually modified to an interest in Law School. Barbara completed a number of independent studies and had an unusual off-campus experience for academic credit.

In one independent study, "Original Ideas in Modern Science Fiction," Barbara read a number of scence fiction works, extracting original ideas and developing social commentary. Barbara read over thirty novels in the course of a semester and received three hours of academic credit. In another independent study, Barbara designed a ten-hour-a-week internship with a local law firm. Her activities included doing legal research and investigation and observation of court activity. She assisted in the preparation of a brief dealing with Alabama's Sexual Psychopath Statute which played a research role in the law eventually being replaced. She received academic credit for her work. In another independent study, Barbara completed a research study on the "Attitudes Toward Women in the Legal System." She developed research which included designing and validating a research questionnaire and administering the questionnaire to three hundred subjects. She analyzed her results and compared them to associated published papers. For this experience she received three hours credit.

The summer before her graduation, Barbara designed an out-of-class learning experience with the Fulton County Juvenile Court in Atlanta, Georgia. The experience involved working as an Assistant Probation Officer in the Dependency and Neglect Division, and as a psychological counselor in the Juvenile Detention Center. The internship was a full-time position and lasted for twelve and one-half weeks. She was assigned her own caseload and did home visits, investigations, and testified in court on behalf of her clients. Barbara received nine semester hours credit for the experience. She has been admitted to Law School.

CASE STUDY NUMBER FOUR

Eddie O'Neil transferred to New College as a sophomore. He had previously been an English major but desired a depth-study which would provide a broader orientation to the Humanities—particularly English, History, and Philosophy. Law School was a definite postgraduate goal so he also needed an acquaintance with the Social Sciences.

New College allowed him to fulfill his Humanities depth-study, primarily in a traditional mode. He took courses ranging from The American Novel and Oriental Philosophy to Accounting and Computer Science. In addition to these regular classroom courses, Eddie completed an independent study entitled "Backgrounds to Literature." In the course of a semester he read various works of Freud, Darwin, Marx, and other social, political, and psychological thinkers who had influenced late nineteenth and twentieth century literature. He met with the instructor every other week. They discussed the readings and their influence on modern writers.

During his junior year Eddie worked for two semesters as an Administrative Intern for the Dean of New College. For these two experiences he received six hours of academic credit. In the course of his internship he became interested in developing new out-of-class learning programs for students at The University of Alabama. He, along with two other New College students, decided to develop a Volunteer Service Bureau for the campus. They decided to work through the University Year for ACTION (UYA) program. UYA is a federal program administered by both New College and the School of Social Work. It allows students to work fulltime off campus on some type of community service project. The UYA students receive academic credit and a cost of living stipend.

Because of the student's efforts, not only was a Volunteer Service Office begun but several new internship programs for credit were started. For his year's experience, Eddie received eighteen hours of academic credit and was able to take a few traditional courses during the year so that he earned a total of a full year's credit. In an evaluation of the experience, he said that he had gained numerous insights into political science, economics and administration. He has since been admitted to Law School.

Dr. Warren Bryan Martin, then Provost of the Old School at Sonoma State College in California, writing in a document for the California Master Plan, stated that, "perhaps the model which contains the largest grouping of significant options for students and changes for faculty is the program of New College, University of Alabama." The New College at the University of Alabama represents a departure from the traditional approach to the undergraduate educational experience at the University and from most institutions nationally.

The New College should be understood as having a two-part mandate: 1) to create an opportunity for a highly individualized approach to undergraduate education utilizing contract-learning which draws freely from the extensive and diverse scholarship of the entire University faculty and from external learning resources, and 2) to serve the University as an experimental unit with the expectation that program concepts, examination and measurement methods, teaching modes, facilities and personnel will provide an experimental base for modifications to other components of the University's undergraduate education programs.

As related to the first purpose of the New College, the individualized curricular approach, there are a number of features of this educational experience which should be mentioned: 1) The use of the learning contract for planning purposes; 2) Admission of a cross section of students with varied educational and vocational goals; 3) A concept of advising that deals with the total development of the individual; 4) A problem-focused approach to general education through interdisciplinary seminars; 5) A recommended out-of-class learning experience for academic credit; 6) The use of depth study programs involving both traditional and non-traditional areas of specialization; and 7) Individualized graduation requirements and evaluation procedures.

The New College is an "administrative college" since roughly two-thirds to three-forths of the student's work is done outside of the New College. Through the New College, students are enrolled in courses from across the University representing any of the various colleges in such a way that educational experiences are packaged to meet students' individual needs. Students are taking course work from all of the various divisions of the University. In this way, students are able to draw on educational experiences from the literally 3,000 course offerings available at The University of Alabama. By individualizing the educational program through the New College, the only additional courses offered are a set of interdisciplinary problem-focused seminars and the opportunity for out-of-class learning experiences. In this way there is no need to completely duplicate faculty and resources already available at the institution. Students receive either a Bachelor of Arts or a Bachelor of Science degree depending upon the area in which they do their depth study, which is a term applied to their area of specialization.

The basic assumptions which underlie the above objectives include the following: 1) That each individual is unique with different needs; 2) That an educational program should be developed which reflects the interests and capabilities of each student; 3) That opportunities should be provided for an individual to be able to learn to think and to deal with principles and concepts rather than simply to memorize data; 4) That students are capable of accepting much of the responsibility for their own learning when given the opportunity to do so; 5) That what someone knows is more important than how they gained that knowledge; 6) That significant learning occurs outside of class as well as within; that is, that learning is not bound by time or place; 7) That problem-focused, general education experiences of an interdisciplinary nature which demonstrate the integration of knowledge are highly desirable in our modern day world; and 8) That part of the role of the faculty member should be seen as that of a co-learner, a mentor in the learning process as well as a source of assistance in the process of acquiring knowledge.

The general context for achieving the goals of the New College is an innovative approach to undergraduate learning. It is important to see the above statement of purpose and basic philosophy in the context of the historical development of the New College idea. For almost a two-year period prior to June 30, 1970, a committee of students, faculty members and administrative members did considerable reading about new forms of learning and visited a number of institutions with innovative programs. The current Dean of the New College served as a consultant to this committee as it began to conclude its work in the spring of 1970 since he had the benefit of major involvement with curriculum development at Ottawa University and had visited a number of innovative colleges as part of a Title III Grant from the Kansas City Regional Council of Higher Education.

In a June 30, 1970 final report, the committee called for a new degree-granting division at the University of Alabama with the following characteristics: 1) Admission based upon demonstrated motivation and intellectual independence with a commitment to a cross-section of students regarding abilities, age, sex and professional or vocational interests; 2) An individualized program of education utilizing the contract model; 3) Unifying study seminars of an interdisciplinary nature dealing with the great and urgent problems of the human condition; 4) An out-of-class learning experience for academic credit recommended for every student; and 5) An opportunity for traditional or non-traditional specialization.

From the beginning, the commitment from key administrators,

particularly from President David Mathews and from Vice-President for Academic Affairs at that time, Raymond F. McLain, was evident. In a June 7, 1971, article about the New College in the "Chronicle of Higher Education," Dr. Mathews is quoted as seeing the New College as a "goad and catalyst for change" in the rest of the institution. The article goes on to say: "The University's President, David Mathews, says that he is committed to reforming undergraduate education, and that the New College seems to be the best way to effect reforms." During the 1970-71 academic year, twenty students were enrolled in the New College as a pilot project group. The current enrollment is approximately 200 students. An additional 150 students are enrolled in some of the programs of the New College even though they are in other divisions of the University. The Sidney A. Mitchell Memorial Fund was established "particularly for the inauguration of the 'New College' program for the students at Tuscaloosa." During the last two years other sources of money from private foundations and federal sources have supplemented the New College budget and have been used for educational development on a University-wide basis.

Features of the Program

Since the New College is not an honors college, the program is available to students representing a wide range of academic backgrounds and levels of intellectual achievement, provided they manifest a significant level of motivation and intellectual independence. An attempt is made with the selection procedures to enroll a representative cross-section of students with regard to such factors as ability, age, sex, race and professional, educational or vocational interests. The following factors are taken into consideration when making a decision for admission: 1) The applicant's self-statement as to why he is interested in the New College and his educational and vocational goals, including any original work by the student; 2) Letters of recommendation (3) from the student's peers and one adult pertaining to the applicant's potential, motivation, strengths and weaknesses, past performance, and personality; 3) An interview with students, faculty and staff of the New College for the purpose of exploring the student's academic objectives and the degree to which the New College can serve him well; 4) Consideration of past learning involvements either from high school or other educational experiences; and 5) Consideration of the ACT score as just another source of information rather than as the primary basis for admission. There are some students in the New College who would not have been admissible to other colleges of the University. Although they appeared to be highly motivated, they had not done well in traditional learning environments. Honor students from high schools are also included in the New College as well as others who performed in an average way although they seem to have the motivation for learning which the Admissions Committee feels is important. There are also a number of adult students in the regular program and a group of adult students who are part of a special external degree pilot project program. The results of all of these efforts to gain information about the applicant are reviewed for a final decision by the Admissions Committee, which is composed of students, faculty and staff of the New College.

The New College provides individualization of curriculum by contractual arrangement with each student. The student, with faculty, community and/or student advisors, plans his program of studies in the context of a Contract-Advising Committee. Usually no more than four individuals serve on this Committee and the only criterion for service is that a particular individual have something definite to contribute to the educational and vocational planning for that particular student. The student's individual needs, desires, capacities, motivations, familial and social influences, as well as his academic performance are taken into consideration by the Contract-Advising Committee. Concern is for the student's total development as a person. The first question on the learning contract is "what are your educational and vocational goals?" This becomes the circumscribing influence for the planning of each student's program. The student assumes the responsibility for getting the advice from members of the Contract-Advising Committee and for entering the material on the learning contract.

The concept of the contract is used to suggest a mutual responsibility on the part of the student and the New College. Regularly updated with the assistance of the Contract-Advising Committee, the graduation contract provides the framework for the educational development of each student in the New College. It is possible to modify the contract every semester or yearly with the approval of the student's Contract-Advising Committee. Final approval of the depth study plan by the New College Review Committee should occur within a year of expected graduation in the event that a student has put together a non-traditional area of specialization. There is an opportunity on the contract for students to note any credit for advanced placement, performance on proficiency exams or demonstrated prior learning experience which has been certified by members of the New College staff. The latter is particularly significant for adult students. Additional information requested on the contract includes plans for an out-of-class learning experience including proposed type of experience, dates, and location, an opportunity to record the main decisions made and areas discussed in each contract-advising session, plans for courses and educational experiences to be taken in the depth study area as well as electives to be added to the student's program. In addition, there is a check-list attached to each contract worksheet which raises a number of questions that the members of the Contract-Advising Committee might want to think about on a fairly regular basis. The members of the Contract-Advising Committee have access to all the informa-tion in the student's file including evaluations from the interdiscipli-nary seminar experiences which provide data of a cognitive, skill, and affective nature. Also included are grades and evaluations from in-class and out-of-class learning experiences as well as a profile for the student from such instruments as the Revised Strong Vocational Interest Inventory if the student has utilized this resource from the Testing Service. The latter information may sometimes be helpful as additional data for the Contract-Advising Committee to have about the student.

Interdisciplinary seminars are offered in the social sciences, the humanities, and the physical and biological sciences. These semi-nars are focused on contemporary problems so as to allow the student to move from knowing to doing, from self-improvement to community betterment. Usually one seminar is taken each semester during the time that a student is enrolled in the New

College. If the student enters as a transfer student, equivalent course experiences may be substituted for some of the interdisciplinary seminars. During the senior year, an opportunity for a multidisciplinary seminar experience for each student is available as a way to synthesize the earlier general education experiences. The seminars, or equivalent educational experiences, are required of all students and run throughout the student's time at the University providing some twenty to twenty-five percent of his educational experience. They also afford a common intellectual experience to foster a sense of community in the New College. In the humanities area, one faculty member provides the continuity for the seminar but persons from on and off campus are brought in to deal with various topics in the course including philosophy, language, painting, sculpture, architecture, music, dance, theatre, and film as varied approaches to the problem of communication in our society. Other seminars deal with such topics as "Human Futures" in the humanities area, seminars on "Man, Behavior and Society" in the social science area, and studying environmental problems such as the Tennessee-Tombigbee Waterway Project in the physical and biological sciences seminar. Regarding the latter example, students might spend part of the semester studying the Army Corps of Engineers reports advocating the Tennessee-Tombigbee Waterway Project and spend the other part of the semester dealing with environmentalist reports as to why this development might cause major problems in the area. In each of the seminar experiences, an analysis of how the various disciplines impinge upon the particular problem under study—history, biology, economics, political science, etc.—provides the basis for class discussion, reading, projects and evaluation activities.

These interdisciplinary, problem-focused seminars are designed to achieve three objectives. First, they are expected to provide the student with an opportunity to gain an understanding of the fundamentals of the main disciplinary areas within the humanities, social sciences, and sciences. Second, they are expected to assist the student in gaining an understanding of the relationships and interdependencies between these and other bodies of knowledge, including those of a vocational nature. Third, the seminars are directly concerned with the great and urgent problems of the human condition, and are designed both to help the student understand these problems and to be effective in responsible relationship to them. Faculty members who provide leadership for the interdisciplinary seminars are on joint appointments between the New College and other divisions of the University.

The concept of the depth-study program corresponds to what is generally considered a departmental "major." The Contract-Advising Committee assists the student with designing an appropriate depth-study program. The usual depth-study program will consist of from ten to twelve courses. Each student is expected to satisfactorily complete the courses and educational experiences which are to be included in his or her particular depth-study program and are agreed upon in the Contract-Advising Committee meeting. In the event that a student wishes to put together a depth-study program which does not fall within a traditional academic discipline, he or she may combine areas of interest and formulate a non-traditional depth-study. Such interdisciplinary approaches to degree programs are encouraged for students whose needs may best be met in this way. These programs are subject to review by a New College Review Committee within one year of graduation. At that time, the student has to explain to a group of three faculty members and one student why they have put together the educational experiences that they have and what they plan to do for the remaining year at the University. All of this is done in the context of the learning contract. Students enrolled in the New College vary in their depth-study programs—from the more usual approaches in such areas as history, elementary education, accounting, or interior design to preparation for higher education administration, pre-law, arts-management or delivery of social services in society. Again, it is the depth-study area which determines whether a student receives a Bachelor of Arts or a Bachelor of Science degree from the University.

Out-of-class learning experiences are encouraged for all students in the New College and are offered on a contract learning basis. In the words of the Carnegie Commission on Higher Education, "much more of education takes place before college, outside of college, and after college than ever before" (Carnegie Commission, 1971). Some of the general purposes for having an out-of-class learning experience include the following: 1) Through out-of-class learning the student will be accorded a variety of learning conditions, and this could be valuable in sustaining his motivation and enthusiasm toward reaching his particular educational goals; 2) The out-of-class learning experience may play an important role in the value development of each student. Once away from the college campus, the student may be better able to question the ideas to which he has been exposed; 3) Certain types of out-of-class learning experiences may encourage each student to gain an appreciation not only of his own culture, but also of other cultures; 4) Each student may gain a more liberal education as the out-of-class learning experience will tend to be highly interdisciplinary, thus bringing to bear areas which a student might not normally think pertinent to his education; 5) Through out-of-class learning the student may be provided the opportunity to earn money at the same time he is gaining practical experience; 6) For the large number of students who are "other-people oriented," the out-of-class learning experience may provide an opportunity to integrate their social concerns with the undergraduate curriculum.

New College encourages its students to pursue their academic interests outside of the classroom through independent study and through out-of-class learning experiences for credit. In both cases learning contracts are used and the student must prepare a clear, concise statement including the course area, topic, or problem he intends to study; his reasons for doing the particular study; his tentative plans for background reading, bibliography, and outline; his plans to initiate the study; and the anticipated outcomes of the study. Independent study options are available in conjunction with either approach to depth study as an additional means by which a student may extend the study of his particular interest. Prior to involvement in independent study, the student must enter into an agreement with a supervising faculty member in such a way that he sets forth his plan for the proposed independent study. Evaluative criteria are established by the student and his instructor prior to the student's receiving a class card for independent study.

Generally, the out-of-class learning experiences are representative of one of five broad categories: (1) Cross-cultural (the student may spend a semester in a foreign country); (2) Sub-cultural (the student may be primarily involved with a cultural group other than his own in this country); (3) Formal employment (the student may work to test his vocational interests); (4) Independent Study (the student may elect to work on a project on or away from campus primarily on his own); and (5) the possibility of credit earned for demonstrated prior learning experiences. Also, out-of-class learning experiences are provided at the undergraduate level through four internship programs. These are in the areas of administration of higher education, college teaching, local business, governmental and industrial agencies, and public service.

The electives program is designed to assist the student in broadening his interests beyond those served by the interdisciplinary seminars and his depth-study program. In the first years at the University, the chosen elective courses may offer the student an opportunity to pursue interests which may become depth-study areas in the future.

In order to graduate from the New College, it is recommended that a student: 1) Take no more than 24 hours of work on the Pass-Fail system without approval of his Contract-Advising Committee (the student is encouraged to take a letter grade option for depth-study courses in light of recent research about graduate school admission preference in one's area of specialization; 2) Have an overall grade average of 1.0 (C) (A = 3.0) for all academic work; and 3) Satisfactorily complete (a) the interdisciplinary general education program or substitute equivalent experience, (b) a depth-study program of either a traditional or a non-traditional nature, (c) elective distribution courses, (d) out-of-class learning experience for credit (highly recommended); and 4) Complete 128 semester hours of work. However, credit for demonstration of knowledge through the College Level Examination Program, proficiency tests, and prior learning experience is possible.

As a response to the growing interest at The University to find ways to meet the special needs of new clientele and in keeping with the experimental mandate of the New College, a planning grant was received from the United States Office of Education— via the Union for Experimenting Colleges and Universities—to explore the use of contract learning in relation to these needs and interests. In organizing the University of Alabama's effort, a planning committee was named that included students, university faculty, homemakers, men in labor and industry, and various community leaders.

There is growing evidence that there will be a "new clientele" in the decade of the seventies which will include those who may be termed "non-traditional." Among this clientele will be homemakers, businessmen, workers and others whose obligations and responsibilities prohibit the expenditure of time required for a traditional college exposure. It was felt that The University of Alabama would be remiss if it did not attempt to find a variety of ways to provide opportunities for these adults and part-time learners. Based on the studies and observations of the External Degree Planning Committee, several recommendations were made such as that the New College should be the agency to develop this experimental program on a pilot basis. The enrollment was limited to those students who are within easy commuting distance of the Tuscaloosa-Birmingham area. It was agreed that the limitations of enrollment and geography would be temporary and would serve only to facilitate internal controls for the program in its early development. The program goals include increasing the opportunities for non-traditional students, through the use of learning contracts; to move toward finding "external" alternatives rather than relying too heavily on "extended" ones; to provide a program in which the student may pursue the B.A. or B.S. degrees; and to experiment with various modes of delivering and evaluating external learning experiences. Students in the program may earn credit for previous learning experiences. The use of the contract learning model for the external degree program not only provides a highly individualized program for students, but it also is in keeping with the University's efforts to extend its resources into the state and to secure greater community involvement in University affairs.

Evaluation of the Program

An unusual paradox of the current concern for reform in higher education is the scarcity of studies of innovation and change. As Mayhew (1971) has said, "Because of student pleas for more relevant education, and because of rather persuasive criticism of the process of education, one would expect a rather rich literature dealing with innovation and experimentation, and it is true that there are descriptions of a number of attempted changes. However, the volume and particularly the EVALUATIVE CONTENT (emphasis added) of these materials is less than could be hoped for. Innovations are apt to be merely described rather than discussed or questioned" (Mayhew, 1971).

If this represents an accurate reading of the literature, then the need for a well-developed evaluation program becomes even more meaningful, not only for the New College, but for other innovative programs as well. In the book *Institutions in Transition* (1971), Hodgkinson, after reviewing the results of the Carnegie Commission on Higher Education's Report for 1970, concludes that . . . a series of federally financed "model colleges" is needed, somewhat akin to the Model Cities program, to try our promising innovation in a variety of institutional settings, with a sophisticated research-and-evaluation component designed into each model college. This is the way to lick the current passivity of institutional responses to new needs—the research and evaluation must be conceived from the ground up as an essential program function (Hodgkinson, 1971b).

One of the most complete reviews of experimental colleges and the problems of research and evaluation is the ERIC Clearinghouse of Higher Education Report entitled *The Experimental Subcollege* (1971). The report indicates that the newly developing subcollege programs attempt to give the student a more personalized environment and to prepare them for the future in new and meaningful ways. These programs are also designed to analyze some of the effects of a "Numbered Society" (student number, social security number, etc.) while hopefully avoiding some of the dehumanizing aspects of a technological society. Consequently, the new programs have a number of common characteristics: 1) They are frequently small relative to other colleges; 2) They offer alternative curricula, many with a liberal arts emphasis; 3) Their educational methods are flexible: independent study; student-formed seminars; community governments; new methods of evaluation; and contract models for assessing student's learning; and

4) They utilize central administrative facilities, usually those of the University.

All students take a standard test battery composed of basic tests administered to all incoming students at the University and a special test battery developed in the New College. This initial testing serves as the baseline against which future testing is compared so that standardized test data can be used to relate New College student development and changes in the general population. The standardized measures consist of the basic University program for all new students—School and College Abilities Test, and American College Test (initial testing only)—as well as the additional New College battery—The Survey of Study Habits and Attitudes, The Omnibus Personality Inventory, The Allport—Vernon-Lindsey Study of Values, and The Revised Strong Vocational Interest Inventory. Basic information about the location of each student is kept after graduation and each graduate has been asked to participate in a follow-up study every three years.

Recognizing that many experiences which may have a significant impact on student development are not necessarily structured learning activities, Berte and Upshaw (1971) suggest that Student Life Studies can identify significant factors in education not measured by traditional tests (Berte and Upshaw, 1971). Consequently, a Student Life Studies Program is a part of the evaluation of the New College. This research approach has been utilized by other institutions with some success. Small groups of students (approximately ten) are randomly chosen from the New College so as to represent all of the interdisciplinary seminars. Similar groups representing the various schools and colleges are randomly chosen from the parent University to serve as a comparison group. Through weekly meetings of small groups of students with faculty, community, or staff persons including Undergraduate and Graduate Interns serving as leaders, data is gathered about experiences students are having and the impact of these experiences on the students' development. Prior to Student Life Studies meetings, the leaders of these groups are assisted in developing their sensitivity to group process and their ability to select details from discussion which seem pertinent to evaluating educational programs.

Leaders spend the first few meetings trying to establish a climate of trust and openness within the group and assuring individual members that their names will not be identified with comments made in the group. The research orientation is stressed so that group meetings do not become "gripe sessions." Rather, a problem-solving, task-oriented approach is used. If someone has a complaint about a particular situation or policy, the group is asked for suggestions or possible improvements. This not only serves to alleviate the "gripe session" atmosphere, but also allows the students to feel more a part of the process of change at the University. Selected group leaders are known on campus as persons who are open to students. So as not to contaminate the research responsibility of the group leader, he or she is encouraged to act as a "participant-observer;" i.e., to encourage students to evaluate their own personal growth and seek to identify possible influences, negative and positive, during their college years. The role of participant-observer is suggested for everyone as an alternative to a role of spokesman for any campus constituency. This helps to facilitate an atmosphere of openness and acceptance within the group (Berte and Upshaw, 1971).

The material is used to implement changes where justified and to provide a basic data bank of relevant experiences in and out of the University community as perceived by students. Student reports on the value of the group are collected and tabulated and referred to appropriate administrative and faculty groups; the results are analyzed in terms of impact on the student and the University and identification of critical factors in behavioral growth and development. The first Student Life Studies Program was conducted during the Spring of 1971. Since then there have been six additional studies. The reports of these studies have been effective in exposing not only areas of needed change but worthwhile accomplishment both in the New College and across the University campus.

As to evaluation of out-of-class learning experiences, any out-of-class learning contract should start with a proposal from the student involved. Included in the proposal from the student should be a section explaining why the out-of-class activity is desirable. A second and highly important section should detail the student's expected outcomes expressed in objective terms. For example, the student should be encouraged to recognize whether this experience would be primarily a source of new information, or perhaps develop needed skills, provide an exposure to his vocational interests, or change his attitude toward or his appreciation for something. As it is quite conceivable that the student may desire to receive credit in more than one academic area, he should decide in what areas academic credit may be appropriate as a part of his proposal. Because of the nature of this type of learning experience, it is recommended that a Pass-Fail grading system be employed for certifying credit although the student may opt for letter grades. In planning the evaluation of the contract experience, the following should be considered: 1) Identification of the person or persons primarily responsible for the evaluation; 2) Record the approximate time the experience will require in number of hours per week if possible; 3) Describe how the experience will be evaluated, e.g., by final product, by periodic evaluations, by project director, by final examination, by the production of a film, work of art, an oral examination, a critical item analysis of journal entries, etc.; 4) The determination of the credit hours to be earned for an experience based upon the duration of the experience, the depth of the experience, and the quality of the experience, (these factors are considered in the process of developing the outline for the experience although they are not finalized until the experience is completed. The typical range of credit for out-of-class learning experiences is one to six hours of credit for experiences done while enrolled in other courses and six to twelve hours for experiences done on a full time basis during a particular semester. There is a general guideline in the New College that approximately ten to fifteen hours of work per week is necessary for receiving three semester hours credit. The students should include a bibliography but they may go beyond this to include other kinds of resources such as persons, places, files and pertinent kinds of hardware or software that might be utilized in the experience. Even though out-of-class experiences are primarily practical in nature, they should include a prominent theoretical element. Often this can be accomplished through related readings—hence the emphasis on the bibliography. If the bibliography is not to be included, the reason for this omission should be given, including the substitute method of including the "prominent theoretical element" or an explanation of why this should not be a part of the experience. Students may arrange for experiences under the direction of persons outside of the University of Alabama who do not have formal academic credentials, but who are highly qualified in a particular area. A procedure has been established whereby certain qualified individuals may be appointed as adjunct faculty of the New College. In order to qualify as an adjunct faculty member, the individual must submit a brief vita or resume indicating his or her expertise in the designated area.

Students who are not formally enrolled in the New College are also able to register for out-of-class learning experiences through the New College. Students may earn financial compensation as a part of their out-of-class learning experience. In these cases it should be clearly understood by the student and his or her employer that the primary reason for the experience is academic and not financial. Faculty members, including adjunct faculty, who have supervised a project or study during an academic year are compensated with a small honorarium per supervised project although the first supervision during an academic year is gratis. It is recommended that any out-of-class learning experience should relate to some facet of a student's regular academic program. Proposals for out-of-class learning experiences which fall into a strict vocational-technical category that do not have a theoretical or academic base are not accepted. The completion of the out-of-class learning contract is the responsibility of the student who is seeking the experience and is generally supervised by a Coordinator of Out-of-Class Learning who is a staff member of the New College.

Another evaluation approach which is utilized is the use of unobtrusive measures. Since the New College has a basic mandate to influence the University in the direction of educational innovation and reform, it is necessary to measure some variables which may not be as apparent as others in terms of evidence of the New College impact on the campus. The following are some examples of indirect measures of possible effects of the New College on the University: 1) Write-ups of the New College in on-campus and off-campus publications such as newspapers, magazines, etc., that the New College does not generate on its own; 2) Faculty applications to teach in the New College; 3) Student applications to enroll in the New College; 4) Requests for catalogs and additional information from students, parents and others external to the New College; 5) Transfers from schools in divisions within the University; 6) Attrition of students, faculty, and staff from the New College; and 7) Visits by representatives of other institutions of higher education and requests for information about the New College.

In an effort to obtain feedback from non-partisan individuals, outside consultants visit the New College on a fairly regular basis. After reviewing available collected data, observing the educational operations, and meeting with students, staff, and administrators, the team submits an evaluation report which is discussed in the context of staff meetings and retreats. This is another source of assessment of the New College Program.

As to the evaluation of faculty members, they are evaluated twice each semester by their students, at mid-term and at the end of the semester. The instructor is rated on a scale which utilizes a continuum with extremes representing least and most desirable characteristics. The qualities evaluated include organization of the seminar, teaching skill, preparation, enthusiasm and interest, quality and reasonableness of assignments, judgement of values, class discussion, and questioning, ability to communicate, mastery of content, integration of knowledge, and the impact of the professor upon the personal growth of the student. Other items on this instrument to evaluate faculty put the students in a position of evaluating their own progress in the course as to the value of this experience and its contribution to the students' vocational, educational, and professional growth. The results of the mid-semester evaluation are made available to the instructor in order that he may make adjustments where appropriate and to indicate to him the students' perceptions of the course at that point in time. The final evaluation by students serves as a basis for an end-of-semester conference between the faculty member and the Dean of the New College for purposes of salary increment, promotion, and tenure consideration. There is some peer interaction among faculty members as another way to provide feedback to the leaders of the interdisciplinary seminars.

In keeping with the contract program and the emphasis on goal development at the New College there is a special assessment instrument for New College faculty and staff known as the Growth Contract. Each semester all members of the faculty and staff (clerical staff included) formulate a Growth Contract as a way to make practical an underlying assumption of the New College, i.e., that faculty and staff members are in a co-learning relationship with students, versus more traditional approaches where the faculty member becomes the primary source for all learning and enters into no agreement to continue his or her own learning. The concept of growth implies change and the idea of a contract connotes a mutual obligation. The following are four elements included in the Growth Contract: (1) Specific goals and plans for action as related to the teaching-learning process. This may include experimentation with new techniques, use of new resources, development of different evaluation approaches, etc.; (2) Growth of a professional nature—readings, development of articles and materials for publication, attendance at various meetings, completion of projects may be considered in this category; (3) Making specific commitments to one's obligations as related to the New College in terms of effective undergraduate teaching, advising, and other research and service activities; and (4) matters related to personal growth and development. Faculty and staff members had an opportunity to evaluate a year and a half's experience with growth contracts and voted to continue this process as a valuable feedback opportunity which encourages self-evaluation and reflection on future directions for one's professional and personal growth.

Faculty members also evaluate student development in each of their seminars. Faculty members are asked to evaluate the students in three areas during the course of the semester. These areas include the cognitive, skill, and affective areas of development. The traditional factors in cognitive taxonomies such as knowledge demonstrated, ability to analyze, critical thinking, ability to synthesize and demonstrate comprehension, etc., are included in this evaluation process. In the skill area, the ability to read, write, use of numbers, etc., are other factors considered. Affective areas which are rated mutually by the student and the faculty member rating the interdisciplinary seminar include motivation, ability to define goals, self-discipline, attitudes, appreciation, ability to evaluate efforts, and social development. The student and faculty member in a one-to-one relationship engage in this kind of evaluation activity at the beginning of the semester and the student and faculty member go through this process again at the end of the semester. These evaluations become a part of the material available to the student's Contract-Advising Committee for purposes of evaluation of the student's performance and development of an educational program on a semester-by-semester basis.

The student, as a member of his Contract-Advising Committee, is involved in the evaluation of his own performance. The Committee provides the student with periodic assessment of his progress towards the previously mutually agreed upon goals. Since all areas of work are reviewed, evaluation for a particular student might involve traditional grading or Pass-Fail options, credit for demonstrated prior learning, advanced placement for degree credit, performance on proficiency examinations, in addition to feedback of various kinds from regular courses taken in the University at large.

During the spring of each academic year, students, faculty and other administrators on the campus have an opportunity to review and evaluate the work of the Dean of the New College. This is done principally through an evaluation instrument which is completed anonymously by the various constituencies served. A three page survey instrument provides an opportunity for the individuals representative of the categories noted above to evaluate the Dean in terms of his general administrative ability, instructional leadership, professional leadership, and personal development. In addition, there are some open ended items which provide an opportunity for people to make comments or recommendations as to how the Dean may more effectively serve the New College, and individuals have an opportunity to express their feelings as to whether or not the Dean should be retained for the coming year.

After the first year of operation, the staff of the New College requested that the President of the University establish a New College Review Committee. This body is composed of faculty members who represent various colleges across the campus and their role is to review any depth-study program that does not fit into traditional disciplinary structures. This Committee represents all colleges of the University and includes students and faculty. The New College Review Committee has been of immeasurable assistance both in formal and informal ways and these individuals have added an element of due process which is an important dimension of the contract-learning process. Students who put together a non-traditional depth-study program have an opportunity to explain within a year of graduation why they have set up the educational experiences that they have as well as to explain what they plan to do for the remaining year and their future plans. Since its inception three years ago, the New College Review Committee members have performed a valuable service of interpretation to other departments and colleges on campus what the mission of the New College is as well as assisting New College students with finalizing their plans for their undergraduate experience prior to graduation.

Conclusion

Based upon four years experience and evaluation data from the various assessment approaches noted earlier, there is substantial evidence that most of the students enrolled in this contract learning program are satisfied with their experiences, basically for three reasons: 1) The feeling that through the contract-advising process that students can turn to competent individuals who care about their educational and vocational future and about them as persons; 2) Their participation in a new form of learning through the interdisciplinary seminars dealing with contemporary problems; and 3) The fact that those students who wish to go on to additional professional or graduate training have not been penalized by virtue of participation in this contract-learning program. More will be said in the concluding chapter about research findings as to what happens to those students who come out of contract-learning programs.

In addition, one of the central purposes of the New College is to serve the University as an experimental base for modifications to undergraduate education. In fulfilling this role, there are a number of developments which have taken place since the New College has been in existence with the following as illustrative:

1) Evidence of more interdisciplinary attempts among departments and divisions on the campus to cooperate with other divisions and through the New College to develop various courses and programs; 2) The creation of a Special Studies Major option in the College of Arts & Sciences which enables the student to individualize their undergraduate experience in a much more flexible curriculum; 3) The adoption of the Internship Program in business-government-industry which was initially established in the New College and taken over by the College of Commerce and Business Administration as well as the offering of other internship programs in other divisions of the University for academic credit; (4) The garnering of federal government and private foundation resources for innovative educational approaches which have been utilized across the University for the benefit of improving the teaching-learning process in a number of ways; 5) The recognition and encouragement of outstanding teaching as the number one priority for promotion and tenure for some faculty members as a policy adopted early by the New College and now accepted by more divisions of the University.

While the New College is certainly not without its difficulties, the use of the contract-learning model has facilitated the individualization of the undergraduate educational experience for a number of students and has contributed to some additional options for teaching and learning on the campus of the University of Alabama.

8 JOHN DULEY

Out-of-Class Learning and Contract Learning at Justin Morrill

There are three basic out-of-class learning opportunities in Justin Morrill College in which contract learning plays a significant role; the *Field Study* program, a term of off campus cross cultural learning, individual *Independent Study* in a particular discipline, and a *Field Education* course in which a group of students undertakes a project in the community under the direction of a faculty member. Three kinds of contracts are used: 1) The Field Study contract focuses attention on the developmental and cross-cultural dimensions of learning and the cognitive is dealt with indirectly or as a derivative of the learning experience. 2) The Independent Study contract concentrates attention on the cognitive, discipline oriented dimensions of learning and encourages the developmental and cross-cultural dimensions to happen without the learner's attention being sharply focused on them. 3) The Field Education contract is developed by a faculty member, or a group of students with a faculty sponsor, and is designed in keeping with the nature of the project, the educational objectives related to a discipline, and the needs and interests of the students.

These offerings differ in their designs but they are undergirded by a common set of philosophical convictions. The central conviction is that learning is most humane and effective when as much responsibility as is appropriate to the readiness of the student is placed upon the learner for the design, development and execution of his own learning experiences with sufficient structure provided

to insure rigorous reflection, quality work, and mutual accountability between learner and teacher. The college believes that under
these circumstances a student will learn to acquire, evaluate,
analyze and synthesize information better, to think more critically,
develop greater creativity and be better able to continue learning
on his own than under circumstances in which it is determined for
the student what and how he shall learn. The college also believes
it is important for students to experience the direct linkage of
theory and practice by practical experience. It is also necessary for
bridges of experience to be provided during a student's academic
life in which the student has the opportunity to test and develop
the skills necessary for the fulfillment of adult roles in society.
Perhaps a wedding needs to be consummated in higher education
between the strong western intellectual tradition of the life of
the mind and the skills and competencies necessary for effective
personal and public life. The first has to do with the development
of intellectual rigor through the mastery of a subject matter area,
the acquiring of cognitive, rational skills and the scientific habits
of mind. The latter requires the development of skills and competencies necessary for a person to function effectively and respon-
sibly on his own and in the sociail environment of others. It is held
that we should assist students in developing the skills necessary for
creative survival and the solution of practical problems in the world
of work and political decisions through the responsible uses of
power and appropriate compromises as well as assist them in the
struggle for objective knowledge and rational system of thought.
In short, we should provide the educational structures in which
students have the opportunity to become "street smart" as well as
"book smart."

The educational opportunities for the application of theory in
practice, for building bridge experiences to adult roles, and for the
balancing of our strong intellectual tradition with cross-cultural
learning may be best provided by the imaginative and responsible
utilization of the larger educational environment of the social,
economic and political structures beyond the classroom. A viable
means of linking together systematic cognitive learning, the student's personal growth and development, and significant involvement in the public realm which we have developed has been the

combined use of contract learning and out of class learning. A contract is understood in this context to be a mechanism for agreement between a teacher and a student or a group of students for the purpose of individualized learning within the expanded learning environment available outside of the classroom. It has been found at Michigan State that each contract needs to include the following elements: 1) A clear statement of the purposes of the project including what the student intends to learn and what he hopes to accomplish in or for the community; 2) A description of the project and the means the student plans to use to carry it to completion; 3) A description of the "out of class" resources which the student will be using and the nature of the involvement in the community which the student will have; 4) A description of the various means which will be used for evaluating the student's work.

FIELD STUDY

The Field Study contract arises out of the necessity to fulfill a college requirement that each student spend a term involved in cross-cultural learning. This program, as with all courses in the College, is evaluated by a Pass-No Credit written evaluation. The written evaluation form contains the following description of the course, its objectives, and the bases of evaluation and is a part of the student's contract:

"This is a program in cross-cultural education involving a three term process of preparation seminar, field study and follow-up seminar. The preparation seminar includes simulated cross-cultural experiences, the development of techniques for learning about communities through a day-in-the-field and follow-up discussion, introduction to values clarification processes, the development of an individualized learning contract, journal keeping and critical incident writing skills focused on cross-cultural learning skills. The student is to keep a journal while in the field and write up 9 critical incidents. The return seminar includes student interviews using values clarification processes in discussing the student's critical incidents and a final paper in which the student reports the results of his field study in terms of his knowledge of another culture, his self-knowledge, and the changes, if any, which the experience brought about in the student's attitudes, values, interests, goals, beliefs or convictions.

OBJECTIVES:

Demonstrated ability in:
1. Writing
2. Information Source Development
3. Cultural Understanding

4. Decision-making
   Demonstrated effort in improving skills in:
5. Interpersonal Communication
6. Commitment to Persons and Relationships
7. Self-understanding and Self-reliance

BASES OF EVALUATION:

1. Critical incidents, final paper.
2 & 3. Day in the Field, presentation, critical incidents, final paper, class participation in Preparation and Return Seminars.
4, 5, 6, & 7. Presentation, critical incidents, final paper, class participation in Preparation and Return Seminars.

Contracts are used in two ways in the Field Study program; 1) as a means of assisting the student in developing his field study project and as a basis for permitting the student to enroll in the course for credit, and 2) to facilitate the student's preparation for his highly individualized project. The contract negotiated with the student before he is permitted to enroll for credit begins to be developed when he first explores with us what he would like to do for his Field Study. As the student begins the process of developing a project or seeking a placement we contract with him to accept any project which he arranges which fulfills the following criteria: 1) The project must provide for in-depth involvement in a foreign culture, a sub-culture in this country, a new role for the student, or a new social setting unfamiliar to the student in which he will not be a casual visitor but an active participant in the daily life and affairs of that social environment; 2) The project must be at least nine weeks in duration; 3) If it is in a foreign country the student must have a two year competency in the language or be willing to attain such competency prior to going on the project; 4) Arrangements must be sufficiently finalized before a staff member will permit a student to enroll for credit. In the event that it is unclear whether or not the project will meet these criteria or can be finally arranged before departure the staff member enters into an agreement with the student to review the project upon the student's return and if it did fulfill the criteria and the student fulfilled the other elements of the contract, he is permitted to enroll for credit and to participate in the follow-up seminar.

The range of options from which a student may choose in arranging his project include: 1) Cross-cultural learning; 2) Occupational exploration; 3) Pre-professional experience; 4) Social action involvement; 5) Service-learning internship. The negotiation of this contract is completed by the end of the term in which the student takes the preparation seminar by his submission and our acceptance of a detailed description of the project for which he had completed the arrangements, a statement of his personal objectives in undertaking this project, his hopes and expectations in regard to the experience. Because of the diverse nature of the projects represented in each preparation seminar, the desire to encourage self-initiated learning, and the differing levels of preparedness of each student, another learning contract is used for the work each student does during the last five weeks of the preparation seminar. The student is asked during the first five weeks of the term, when the seminar is meeting weekly, to develop a learning contract describing what he plans to do during the balance of the term to prepare himself to maximize his learning while involved in the Field Study. This contract is reviewed by the seminar leader, suggestions made for modification, and returned to the student with a copy being kept by the instructor. At the end of the term, with the paper finalizing his contract for the Field Study assignment, the student submits a progress report on this learning contract.

One of the positive values of the Field Study initiating contract is that it allows the student to design or select projects, with faculty advice, that are consistent with his needs, interests and readiness to venture into the unknown. The range of projects in which students engage includes established group programs that require very little initiative on the part of the student such as those conducted by the Volunteers for International Development or the Experiment in International Living, to individual projects designed and executed by the student such as that of the student who was a participant/observer with the Revolutionary Left in Ireland or the experience of four students who purchased, reconditioned and sailed the *Neith,* a 1908 Herschoff designed 53-foot sailing ship from Falmouth, England to Palma, Spain and Antigua in the Caribbean Sea, and include more moderately demanding experiences such as serving as a volunteer in an orphanage in Honduras, or teaching English as a second language in Mexico City.

On the negative side, the fact that the responsibility for the selection or development of the project is an individualized contract becomes a serious barrier for some students who are inexperienced in accepting responsibility for their own lives. It would be much easier for these students to become involved if the college would organize group cross-cultural projects in which 20 to 30 students from the College would participate. The placing of full responsibility upon the student for the initiation and execution of the project provides such diversity that it is difficult for the staff to assist the student in taking maximum advantage of the learning potential of each project. Previously the only mechanisms which were used for structured reflection upon the experience were the student's journal, an oral presentation in the follow-up seminar and a final paper in which the student reported what he learned from the experience. The quality of the reflection depended almost entirely upon the quality of the student's journal. With the introduction of identified cross-cultural learning skills and the Critical incident Technique a sharper focus has been provided, yet the flexibility of the open choice of the project has been maintained. The student has been given a more structured means for reflection as well as a more clearly defined purpose for keeping a journal. The student is still required to keep a journal and to write a final paper reporting the learning which took place, using the critical incidents as supportive evidence.

The fact that the preparation seminar is a non-credit course taken while carrying a full academic load means that the learning contracts developed by students in that seminar, to be used during the rest of the term, are very uneven in quality. Their quality is dependent upon the degree of commitment the student has to his project and his capacity to imagine what would be most helpful as preparation for the experience. The learning contract does perform an integrative function in that the student is asked to indicate in the contract what past and present courses are seen by him as preparatory for his Field Study. The means of evaluation used in this program are the student's own reporting of his experience through his journal, oral presentation, paper and critical incident writing and the staff member's observation of the student over the three term period in which the student is involved. Some standardized approaches to measure values and attitudes before and after the experience are being designed.

The following reports give some evidence of the effectiveness of this contractual design for individual students. A pre-medical student in the College developed a contract in which he spent his field study living with families and working as a para-professional with two General Practitioners in two economically different areas of the state for equal periods of time. The doctors themselves were very different. One was an older man with an established practice who conserved his psychic resources. The other was a young man with a very sensitive social conscience who spent himself without counting the cost to his personal health or family relationships. Besides developing cross-cultural learning skills, the student confirmed his interest in medicine as a profession and upon his return to campus became deeply involved in the medical work of the Drug Education Center and became a trained counselor in the local Problem Pregnancy Counseling Program. This service involvement was, according to his final paper, the direct result of the field study experience. The contractual nature of this program made this unique placement possible and built into it the reflection which led to his service involvement.

The crew of the *Neith,* referred to earlier in this chapter, took an agonizingly long time to complete their contract because of their difficulty in conceptualizing what they knew to be extremely important learning for them. They wrote in their final paper: "We confronted our Mediterranean situation, and it became very apparent that we could not fulfill our original MSU study agreements. They were to be highly structured sociological, anthropological, and geographical investigations of cities adjoining the harbors we visited.* Our actual problems, as opposed to these

---

*Because they were to be gone more than one term, they developed some Independent Study Contracts in addition to their Field Study Contracts.

scholastic ones, were omnipresent and left time for little but their solutions. Realistically, our nautical-type environment required that we direct our total efforts towards survival. The cities for us became sources of food, fuel, supplies, equipment, and repair facilities. In short, they were tools to be used to help replenish the self-contained systems which were necessary for our survival. In Palma we worked constantly, and the "Neith" was brought successfully to a high level of readiness. As the months of August and September passed, we began to take more pride in the "Neith" as she neared "yacht finish." She became more and more seaworthy as her systems (lighting, propulsion, protection, communication, maintenance, etc.) were brought up to their maximum possible level of performance. With her increased sea capabilities she would be able to control or divert the energies encountered in most foreseeable circumstances.

"On November 28, 1970, we set sail for 'the land of the free and the home of the brave.' Twenty-eight days would pass prior to our next landfall. The first 20 days of the 3500 mile passage were slow, sunny, and easy. During the frequent periods of calm, we read books and swam under the hot tropical sun. This became the most significant part of the trip. During it we each realized an immense potential to our individual awarenesses and capabilities. This discovery, which was undeniably the most important of the trip, was a collective one. We all enthusiastically discussed it, how the previous nine months of hard work and self-discipline naturally snowballed to this point. Our specialized environment demanded and exercised the full spectrum of our potential. Although many books were read at this time it never bore any resemblance to a "scholastic" learning experience. The effect of the boat was to bring forth full access to all previous experience. The most comprehensive books we had thus far read in our lives were absorbed while being able to interrelate all previous knowledge immediately. The phenomenon was so astounding that we came to the conclusion that this must be what passes for "higher consciousness."

"In this state of mind great things seemed possible. It was as though we could comprehend the accomplishments of great men, because we were looking from the same hilltop. Unexpectedly, people widely separated by time, place, and disciplines were found to be united by foundations. Comprehensiveness gave rise to immense energies, and it no longer seemed a mystery how major works were accomplished. We were still isolated in the Atlantic and wondered to each other if what was happening could be brought back into the world we had left a year before. The change we encountered upon returning to school was much less of a problem than we had anticipated. We had been told to expect a shock upon re-entering college life, but it surprisingly did not occur. The college routine seemed like a pleasantly simple game from what we had left. We realize now why this was true. Other people with field study experiences became more specialized in coping with their study environments. They merely had to discover where and how to plug themselves into static existing environments. Upon return they found it difficult to change from one specialized way of life to another. In contrast, our trip led to a more generalized and comprehensive dynamic understanding, which enabled us to cope with the static, specialized environment we returned to."

One of the crew summed up this change in their way of thinking in this way. "One of the most important single things I have learned after sailing 11,000 miles is the concept of "comprehensive thinking." I describe it as thinking of a system as a whole rather than as a group of separate parts. In this way, I seem to get a view of the entire scope of a particular problem, not just any one aspect; it is the discovery of the underlying fundamental principles which gives me a total outlook on a situation." In that paper he goes on to explain the profound effect that the trip had on his life and work.

A student who had no clear occupational goals or much sense of direction in her life, as is true of many students, arranged a field study in a settlement house in Liverpool, England through the Winant Volunteers. According to her journal and her final paper she spent most of the first part of her time in Liverpool bitterly complaining to herself and others about the family she lived with and the way they treated her, about the incompetence of the man she worked for and the bad condition of the center and its facilities. In short, she was prevented from doing or learning very much by her very negative, fault finding attitude. In the course of her third week there she ran into a young American woman who had lived in Liverpool for three years and was working in a youth program which she and some English young people had created out of their own resourcefulness and resources. They were living from hand to mouth to keep it going. This meeting became a dramatic encounter for the student in which she recognized what she had been doing. She quit complaining, linked forces with these people and did a remarkable piece of work in the settlement house she was serving. In the follow-up seminar it became evident she was having a serious re-entry problem, in fact she had struggled for a long time while in Liverpool with the question of whether or not she ought to stay there. On her return to Michigan State she discovered how much it meant to be needed, counted on and responsible to and for other people. She had experienced that in-depth for the first time in Liverpool and upon her return to MSU she rediscovered that it did not matter to anyone whether she was there or not or whether she did anything or not. The experience she contracted for and the reflection built into the contract forced her to do some deep and hard thinking about herself, the influence of her attitudes on her behavior, her values and what she wanted to do with her life. It also demonstrated to her that she could function effectively under strange and adverse circumstances, giving her more confidence in herself than she had before.

A pre-law student who appeared to have had considerable work experience and had demonstrated abilities to function on his own in new social environments had delayed doing his Field Study until his Senior year. A number of possible contracts were explored including a placement as an aid to the Senate Administrator in the State Senate of Oklahoma, an internship in HEW, an internship with the State Legislature of Maryland and work in a Legal Aid Office. Arrangements were finally completed for placement in a Legal Aid Office in Atlanta, Georgia. Because finalization of the placement was delayed for so long, no learning contract was developed or worked on during the preparation seminar. Basically the student's attitude throughout the preparation seminar was that he had a requirement to fulfill for graduation and he would do it. He survived the term in Atlanta and dutifully did what was asked of him at the Legal Aid Office but he did not, by his own admission, learn anything he did not already know about himself, the environment in which he served, or the legal profession as it expresses itself through such offices. The contract did not assist this student in making this a learning experience nor did it help us in assisting him in reflecting on why it was not a learning experience for him.

The practical realities of the use of the Field Study contract have recently been highlighted. The College has just been evaluated under the regular procedures of the University for the periodic review of Colleges, Schools and Departments. As a result of that evaluation and the growing financial crisis in higher education one of the recommendations is that by 1976 the College be producing 900 credit hours per fulltime faculty member. The Field Study Office is staffed by 1½ positions which means that in order to fulfill our minimal responsibility by 1976 we must produce 1450 credit hours or oversee the projects of 121 students during the course of each year. During the present year we have had approximately 85 students in the field which means we shall have to increase the number of students involved by 36. The other alternative, of course, is to reduce the staff by ½ a position but the nature of the program could not be maintained if that were done. In order to become financially feasible we shall have to increase the enrollment in the College, or increase the number of non-JMC students served by the program, or reduce the number of students doing Independent Study in place of Field Study or some combination of these three.

One of the faculty development needs in this program is for the staff to develop as wide an acquaintance with the alternative possibilities for field study as possible. This means continually exploring new service-learning internships, voluntary service possibilities, archaeological digs, explorations, and expeditions. The faculty and staff must also continue to develop creative skills in interacting with students on a one to one basis to discover their interests, assess their level of readiness for venturing into the unknown, and in exploring the options they may wish to investigate. Given the normal barriers between persons, the generation gap, the usual image of the professor as an authority figure, the anxiety producing nature of spending a term off campus on your own in a strange environment, and other impediments to interpersonal communication, the creation of a climate of free and open exchange is a task requiring considerable skill and conscious effort. This skill development is especially important in connection with the student who wishes to create his own field study project.

FIELD EXPERIENCE WITH A DISCIPLINE

The second and third types of out-of-class contract learning, *Independent Study* and *Field Education,* are related to the process of field experience within a discipline. Learning experiences occur in the field in which the scope, language, concepts, assumptions, theories, methodologies and knowledge of various disciplines is learned and utilized in relation to the consideration of a specific issue or topic in the field. There are three distinctive elements of this out-of-class contract learning experience: 1) The work done in the field is related to a discipline; 2) It is under the supervision of a faculty member who is a representative of that discipline; 3) The student's work is accepted for credit on the basis that it demonstrates the knowledge or mastery of an aspect of the discipline which was contracted for by the student and the sponsoring faculty member.

Both field discipline oriented contracts arc initiated in a variety of ways. Independent Study is initiated by a faculty member by requiring individuals to undertake field projects as part of a course. Field Education or group contracts for field projects are initiated by faculty when a faculty member designs a course around a community problem he has identified in cooperation with community people for the purpose of teaching about his discipline and serving the community through the work of the class. Independent Study projects are initiated by students when a student devotes a whole term to an in-depth study in the field, or a student, while taking a particular course, develops an interest in an issue in the community which is related to the work of the course. Another option is that a student, while on his field study, develops a proposal for the study of an aspect of that culture using the tools of a particular discipline. Field Education or group projects are initiated by students when a group of students identify a problem or issue in the community about which they wish to undertake action/research using the tools of a particular discipline.

While a rich diversity of ways of initiating these projects is fostered in the College, the process utilized in carrying them out is similar. With the student initiated projects, the student or group of students must develop a proposal setting forth what is to be done, and on the basis of that proposal, secure the sponsorship of a faculty member. Together with the faculty sponsor they refine the proposal so that it clearly states: 1) The educational and task objectives that are to be accomplished; 2) The focus of the study; 3) The techniques to be used; 4) The nature of student involvement; 5) The community resources to be utilized; 6) A description of the process by which the project will be carried out and monitored by the faculty sponsor; 7) The basis on which the project will be evaluated and credit granted. As the projects develop the contracts may be modified by mutual agreement between the faculty sponsors and the students. With faculty initiated projects the contract is developed by the faculty member as part of the design of a course and the student involves himself in the contract as a part of his participation in the course. The same elements are included with these contracts as with the student initiated ones.

The criteria for accepting or rejecting projects include an assessment by the faculty as to the readiness of the student to undertake the project, the adequacy of the design to provide sufficient involvement in the discipline to warrant the awarding of academic credit, the amount of work involved, the time available for its accomplishment, and the clarity and completeness of the proposal.

INDEPENDENT STUDY

Descriptions of two uses of Independent Study contracts follow: 1) The first deals with a political science course which is offered during election years that is focused on the American electoral process. The course involves both a weekly seminar and field experiences. The objectives of the course were that each student demonstrate: 1) an understanding of the electoral process through involvement in it; 2) an understanding of the impact of the political issues of the campaign on the candidate and the electorate, and 3) the ability to use the methodology and insights of Political Science through an analysis of the trends and possibilities of the election.

The objectives were defined by the instructor with students developing individual contracts for meeting the objectives. The individual contracts detailed the specific means by which each student agreed to an involvement in the subject matter and in the political process. Students were encouraged to include direct involvement within a political campaign in their contracts either at the local, state or national level and in whatever aspect of the campaign they wished to be involved. Each contract included a component based on the totality of the experience in which an analysis or interpretation of the experience demanded an interaction between the affective and the cognitive dimensions. Evaluation was based on demonstrated evidence of the student's involvement in the political process and understanding of the discipline of Political Science. Throughout the course the faculty monitor remained in close touch with the students as a resource person, utilizing the seminars to provide information and the opportunity for students to share with and to assist and encourage one another.

2) A number of students while doing their field study in a different cultural setting have developed Independent Study contracts in order to study selected aspects of their field study environment, utilizing the concepts and insights of a particular discipline. These contracts are developed in detail and include some work in preparation for the field involvement. The student is expected to demonstrate some mastery of the concepts before departure since the supervisor would not be available in the field. It is understood, however, that the experience itself will provide the means for further clarification and verification of the concepts at issue. Effective use of this model has been demonstrated by students focusing on the processes of political and economic development in such countries as Columbia, Greece, Brazil, and Tanzania. Variations have permitted contracts in the process of community development within the Model Cities programs of Lansing, Michigan and Atlanta, Georgia.

An analysis of the effectiveness of the independent study contract indicates that these contracts have enabled students to pursue their individualized interests and have encouraged a higher degree of motivation and interest than might otherwise have been present in the usual structure of a course setting. Many faculty members have made these learning experiences high points in the academic experiences of students by their mutual involvement with the student in his creative struggle to master some aspect of a discipline in the accomplishment of a clearly defined and specific task. The excitement graduate students and their faculty mentors experience on the frontiers of knowledge are often mirrored in the undergraduate's Independent Study experience under a wise, sensitive, and creative faculty sponsor.

The strength or weakness of this form of learning, as in all forms, is determined by the people involved. It is a highly demanding mode for both students and faculty and when it is undertaken by a faculty member who is unable to give care and attention to the refinement of the contract and the monitoring of the learning process, the result for the student is a project in which few relationships are established between the work done and the focus, language, concepts, assumptions, theories, methodology and subject matter of the discipline. These connections are difficult enough to establish at best and without a mutuality of involvement on the part of student and his sponsor there is very little chance that they will happen. Much of the Independent Study undertaken is supervised by faculty as an overload and therefore the time and energy to do it well are not available. The line of least resistance for a faculty member confronted by an interested student with a rough draft of a proposal is to accept the initial proposal with a few modifications and to evaluate the work if and when it is submitted. With a student already well experienced in Independent Study and well grounded in a discipline such an experience can be educationally beneficial but for the student who is uninitiated in the rigors of Independent Study and the workings of the discipline, he often flounders and fails to complete the project.

In the experience of the College, there are too many Incomplete grades given in Independent Study projects. The incompleted Independent Study projects should never have been undertaken for any one of a number of reasons. They were either too ambitious in contract design, setting up objectives which could not be accomplished within the time constraints of the study, or the student was not trained enough in the discipline or experienced enough in working independently to carry out the project, or the faculty had insufficient time to provide the necessary support system for the student. More viable contracts would be designed and responsible relationships established between students and sponsors if a college review committee were established to approve all Independent Study projects which are for 6 or more credits. This would provide a framework for consistency of quality and protect faculty from their tendency to over extend themselves in responding to the individual requests of students.

We have done no research comparing the effectiveness of Independent Study in the field with classroom learning but it is clear that contracts are very effective facilitators of learning when the project is of limited enough scope that it can be accomplished through the given skills of the student in the time available. An Independent Study contract can be an effective learning device if the objectives are clearly stated, and if the process by means of which the student is going to do the project is carefully developed, described, and monitored by the sponsor.

FIELD EDUCATION OR GROUP PROJECTS

The following are examples of Field Education or group contracts. 1) The initiative for one field education project came from a group of several students, encouraged by a County Mental Health Coordinator. The project was to investigate the apparent disproportionate use of funds among the three counties participating in joint programs. In a meeting with the official and the students, the faculty sponsor agreed to supervise the project provided it was expanded to include a study of the decision making processes at the tri-county level regarding mental health programs with an analysis of possible adjustments in those processes under pending revised revenue sharing programs. The original project failed when the initiating students did not enroll for credit. Several new students agreed to contract within the suggested objectives for a parallel experience. The resulting contract was between these students and the faculty sponsor, with a further expansion in the frame of reference. The students desired to examine the state legislation, undergoing revision at that time, which authorized and controlled county mental health programs. They agreed further to

interview State Legislators, County Commissioners, Mental Health
Board Members, and County Co-ordinators and Directors before
filing a report. The project became a study of intergovernmental
relations in the area of mental health.

2) A faculty member received a request from the Director of
the Model Cities Program of the City of Lansing to assist his staff
by finding out for them the levels of understanding and commitment of the various publics involved in the Model Cities Program.
A Field Education project was initiated by two faculty members
in response to their request. Twenty-two students were involved in
the program as an introduction to Political Science in the context
of Urban Development. The central core of the course was a survey
of the understanding and attitudes of community leaders and
participants concerning the Lansing Program. The first phase
involved the students in a process of identifying influential community leaders. A special team of students surveyed a random
sampling of Lansing citizens from business, labor, industry, education, religion, social services and the mass media. From the initial
survey, those persons mentioned most frequently as influential
community leaders were interviewed as to their knowledge of and
attitude towards the Lansing Model Cities Program. Along with
these thirty-five identified community leaders, seventeen members
of the Policy Board of the Program, one City Councilman, and
eighteen elected members of nine Task Forces were interviewed.
Three parallel questionnaires were developed by the students for
use in interviewing. A final report of the findings of the class was
developed and submitted to the Director of the Program for use
with his staff. The execution of the course required the students
to develop knowledge of the enabling Federal legislation estab-
lishing the Model Cities Program, and of intergovernmental relations as they are expressed in Federal, County and municipal
cooperation in programs like Model Cities. Subcontracts for
various aspects of the work were developed within the class. In
this example problem identification, program design, development
and execution were faculty responsibilities. Students participated
in shaping the program through identifying influential persons in
the community, developing and refining the questionnaires, con-
ducting the interviews and assisting with the preparation of the

final report. This was clearly a faculty initiated Field Education program.

The analysis of the effectiveness of the use of Field Education contracts in the College is done in two parts: faculty initiated contracts and our attempts to encourage and facilitate student initiated contracts.

Faculty initiated Field Education contracts have been highly successful when the initiating faculty member or staff member has had good credibility and extensive contact in the community; has been interested in developing Field Education courses in his discipline for groups of students and in using his discipline to help community people solve their problems. This type of learning contract requires faculty with unique skills. There are two things the teacher is trying to do: work with the students within a community setting to complete a project and through that experience to teach the students something about the discipline. To teach students a discipline in the controlled situation of the classroom with a pre-planned syllabus is difficult enough, but in the community project setting it has to be done often on the run and in the midst of unexpected developments or crises and the ever present pressure of time. It requires of a person the double vision of keeping one eye on the project and the other on the look-out for opportunities to demonstrate the ways in which the discipline can be related to the project instructionally. It requires that there be consciously built into the experience the provision of basic information about the discipline, its scope, concepts, methodology, knowledge base, as well as key points at which the discipline's relevance to the issues at hand are demonstrated. When these skills are present, it makes for an excellent learning experience, giving students the opportunity to relate theory and practice and assists them in experiencing new adult roles in service in the community.

In regard to the effectiveness of student initiated Field Education or group contracts, a brief history of its development in the College is needed in order to understand it fully. In the Spring of 1970, in response to increased student interest in the shaping of their own education and in an effort to expand the number of community-based learning experiences, the College created the Field Education Program in Public Affairs and the Arts to facilitate group contracts for learning experiences in the field. An Advisory Board was created for this program which was made up of 2 faculty members, 2 students, and 2 people from the public realm— a member of the State House of Representatives from the westside of Lansing and a Lansing high school teacher and County Commissioner who was deeply involved in community organizing. The development of group contracts and the execution of projects was a three term process. An issue was identified by students in the College with assistance from the Advisory Board, the proposal developed and the faculty sponsor secured during the first term. During the second term the students and the faculty member refined the contract (developed the course syllabus, completed the design of the project, secured the community resources, worked out the educational process, determined the bases of evaluation, and recruited the other students). During the third term the project was carried out. A number of problems surfaced in the execution of this design. The Advisory Board developed a list of community issues and needs and the Field Education staff member sought to recruit students to develop proposals for courses. The fact that someone else had identified the issues meant that students were being recruited to carry out someone else's suggestions. The lack of knowledge of and involvement in the community on the part of students meant that the students were not interested in many of the issues or aware of other viable ones. An additional problem arose in that once an issue was identified and developed into a course by a small group of students and a faculty member, there was often not sufficient interest on the part of other students to justify offering the course.

For the Winter term two appropriate courses were developed from the list suggested by the Advisory Board: a course in community organization related to volunteer service in the Chicano community in Lansing and a course in County Government in which a citizen's manual of County Government, its services and resources was developed. The other courses the students chose to develop for the first term were not discipline oriented field experiences: a course in psychology, assisting in the processing of research data which had been gathered on Shock Therapy, and one in Social Psychology on intentional communities.

With an Education Development Program grant provided by the Office of the Provost at Michigan State University, a new format was tested in 1972-73. The purpose of the new design was to counteract the limitation of the lack of knowledge and involvement in the community by students and the limited faculty resources in the College and to test the idea for wider usage in the University. A group of students was recruited from among upperclassmen who had worked in the Lansing area through the MSU Volunteer Bureau. These students were to work with the Field Education staff person to identify a community project on the basis of their experiences and contacts in the community, design it, determine the skills and knowledge they needed to carry out the project, contract with University faculty members for Independent Study to gain these skills, share them with other project members through a seminar, and carry out the project. The role of the staff member was as educational facilitator to the project and to evaluate the work of the students.

The project failed for a number of reasons. The issue identification stage of the project was very time consuming and frustrating. It took a lot of meetings and interviews with community contacts to identify an issue. The issue of health care delivery services on the northside of Lansing was finally identified as an issue the students and community people were interested in. As the work progressed on the development of the project the students began the design of a research project which the community people rejected because they wanted help in engaging in confrontation politics. The students withdrew from that involvement on the basis of being unable to make the time commitment necessary to see such a project through and being unwilling to get involved in that way in the community. At this point a request came from students to serve as aids to Spanish speaking families to help them in their efforts to function in the community and the students decided to drop the project and work with the families, each doing an Independent Study in relation to his work with the families.

EVALUATION OF THE FIELD EDUCATION
PROGRAM IN PUBLIC AFFAIRS AND THE ARTS

The following conclusions have been drawn from the College's four year involvement in efforts to provide the maximum opportunity for groups of students to participate in the development of community based learning experiences by means of contracts developed with faculty sponsors.

1) The particular design of the Field Education Program in Public Affairs and the Arts was inappropriate in that it contained too high an expectation in regard to the capability of undergraduate students. It went too far in placing responsibility on the students to do the initial identification of issues or projects in the community and to develop the original proposal upon the basis of which a faculty sponsor was recruited. In those incidents in which project identification and the initial design of the learning experience was done by a faculty or staff person, students were able to participate creatively in the refinement of the group contract and the negotiation of options for sub-groups in the course.

2) The original design was also inadequate in that the length of time required in the program to identify an issue, develop a contract with a faculty member, prepare and offer the course was too long (three terms) to sustain the interest and involvement of students.

3) This is an expensive method of teaching. The number of students who can be worked with in such student initiated experiences is limited and it does not lend itself to high credit hour production.

THE IMPLICATIONS AND FURTHER USEFULNESS
OF OUT OF CLASS CONTRACT LEARNING

The element of greatest educational significance in out of class contract learning is the fact of mutuality. Because the student is mutually involved with a faculty member in the design and implementation of his own learning he has a different kind of relationship with his teacher than a student in a classroom setting. His situation changes from being a complying participant in someone else's educational design to being an active agent involved with another person in the creation of the design for his own learning. His situation changes from being a receiver of information to being a person to be guided in self-initiated inquiry. The mutual involvement is an important expression of trust and confidence in the judgment and maturity of the learner. Such mutuality recognizes sound judgment and maturity when it is warranted and strengthens the learner's positive feelings about himself. This mutuality acknowledges the student's value as a person and provides a learning environment which frees him to express his individuality positively while at the same time holding him accountable for responsible work.

There are three other factors worthy of note in out-of-class contract learning. The student is provided with the opportunity to test out adult roles under supervision and to see the connections between theory and practice in controlled circumstances. The traditional conditions of rigorous reflection and quality work are maintained in these programs but in an atmosphere that provides for individuality in intellectual growth and development. In the light of the experiences described in this chapter there are four major areas for which out of class contract learning has implications: competency based degree programs, life long learning, the granting of credit for life/work experience, and the improvement of cooperative education and career exploration opportunities. There is a persistent restlessness among educators with the model of undergraduate education whose main components consist of a fixed amount of time spent in an institution, the time being used in rather rigidly predetermined ways: primarily in blocks of time of eleven or sixteen weeks with the student mastering the content of certain subject matter areas and being required to demonstrate retention powers and thought processes in using it in a narrow way, i.e., a final exam. Despite its limitations, this process has served society well. A number of people have learned to learn by means of this process and the ongoing work of our society is being carried out by those educated in this way. The current concern of educators is to improve the system so that the main purpose of a liberal education and use of its resources and talents can be concentrated on teaching people how to learn and launching them on an ongoing life of inquiry.

9 JOHN BILORUSKY AND HARRY BUTLER

Beyond Contract Curricula to Improvisational Learning

In the past few years, students and faculty at many institutions of higher education have attempted to develop curricular innovations which individualize learning. However, the intentions of many faculty and students, including the authors, have very often been frustrated by the structural constraints of the curricula in which these innovations have been tried. For example, when students enroll in a student-initiated course which is graded on a pass-fail basis, the pressure of grades in the students' other courses usually diverts their energies from the pass-fail course. Similarly, an instructor's desire to encourage students to pursue independent research projects in his classes may be thwarted by the length of the class. It is difficult for students to formulate and implement a major project in 10 weeks, especially when they are enrolled in several other classes. Indeed, seemingly radical changes in curricula have often failed to nurture student initiative and alter the authoritarian nature of the "hidden curriculum" (cf. Snyder, 1971; Pear, 1970; Illich, 1971).

Experiences such as the above led the authors to believe that completely new curriculum structures are needed to enhance student learning in general and student autonomy in particular. Consequently, while members of the faculty of the College of Community Services at the University of Cincinnati, the authors formulated an alternative curriculum structure, called the Individualized Learning Program (ILP). The ILP was proposed in November 1971. About 20 students and four faculty were actively involved in planning the program during the winter and spring of 1972, and the program began operation the following fall. There were

144

31 self-selected participants enrolled in the ILP during 1972-73, majoring in social work, criminal justice, urban affairs, and community services. Students in the ILP, like all of the (approximately 500) undergraduates in the College were juniors or seniors. The ILP student body was diverse in terms of student backgrounds and ages. A dozen faculty, a large majority of the faculty in the two-year old College, served as advisors as an unpaid overload during the first year of this curricular experiment.

Each student in the ILP planned his program with the assistance of an advisory committee selected by the student. The committee included at least two faculty from the College, and sometimes students and community people were added to the committee. The student and his committee determined collaboratively each student's program of learning. The responsibility for generating proposed learning directions rested with the individual student, but the committee was available to give guidance and assistance. Student programs were developed from many arenas of experience: internships or field placements; independent study; student-initiated courses, study groups, or action groups; participation in or observation of lectures, panels, discussions, meetings, and workshops in the community and the university; and only occasionally, courses in this and other colleges.

Each student was responsible for evaluating the quality of his learning experiences. Students received pass-no pass grades for each quarter's work. Each student prepared a file of evidence of learning or a learning portfolio. Through the portfolio, the student demonstrated and explained the processes as well as the products of his learning. Students were encouraged to give special consideration to the processes of integrating theory and action. (The learning portfolios will be discussed in greater detail in the section on learning-certification contradictions.)

AN EMERGING THEORY

The authors' experiences with the ILP were very encouraging; student learning did seem to be greatly enhanced by this approach. And, as a result of these experiences, the authors learned much about the learning process. Most importantly, we began to learn how to make critical comparisons of significant, but often subtle, differences among many approaches to individualized learning. We learned to perceive certain *patterns* of educational strategies (regarding student-faculty relations, advising practices, use of learning portfolios, etc.); we noted that these patterns seemed to form internally consistent "gestalts." We began to appreciate and understand the implications of these different patterns by reflecting on our educational practices with different students, by spending many hours discussing and comparing our practices with each other, and by observing the practices of other faculty (including those reported in publications on higher education, such as *Change*).

We finally conceptualized these patterns of educational strategies as four curricular models. These models are conceptualized as a hierarchy according to their degree of openness, and the extent to which they allow and encourage the development of student autonomy: the performance model (which is exemplified by most college curricula), closed and open contract models, and the "experimenting community" (which nurtures improvisational learning). Moreover, these curricular models are seen as examples of social systems or organizations which may be parallel to the stages of human development found in the theories of Loevinger (1970) and Kohlberg (1971). Both are stage theorists who use a cognitive-developmental approach to the study of the socialization of man. This theoretical perspective suggests the importance of studying interrelations between conceptual arenas which are all too often seen in isolation from each other: curriculum building, human development and learning, social systems and organizations, and visions of man-and-society.

To be sure, these four curricular models may seldom occur in their "pure" forms. Elements and strategies from different models are often mixed in everyday practices. For example, comments at the beginning of this article suggest that when a strategy of a more open model is used in the context of a more closed curricular structure, the effectiveness of the more open strategy is often severely limited. However, it may be quite possible to integrate elements from different models. In fact, the authors believe that no degree-granting curriculum could be an exemplar of an "experimenting community," and the ILP can be viewed as an attempt to synthesize aspects of the open contract and experimenting community models.

We propose these four models as guides or preliminary frames of reference for critically examining and using different strategies for individualizing education. These concepts are grounded in our experiences with the ILP. However, we do not propose these models (and the implied hierarchy of models) as a substantiated theory. We look at the models as a reasonable, somewhat empirically validated, starting point for thinking about and practicing individualized education. The principal challenge projected by this article is for all of us, readers and authors alike, to now try to apply this theory to our educational practices and to critically evaluate and modify the theory in light of those applications.

FOUR CURRICULAR MODELS

Traditional curricula, which emphasize conformity, are here conceptualized as "performance models." These curricula reflect Loevinger's conformity stage in rule orientation, faculty and administrative authority, and the duty nature of study. The conformist's search for right answers and true theories is reinforced by the instructor's standards of performance, which include memorized responses on tests. Evaluation is manifested in grades and approval from others, mainly faculty and supervisors. Faculty-student interactions are characterized by authoritarian relationships in that students are excluded from the evaluation process. Faculty authority and student passivity are inherent in the performance model. The certitude underlying the performance model is manifested in prepackaged curricula. The package preconstructs content, time, and style of interaction. The predictability and concreteness of this prepackaging provides students, faculty, and administrators with a measure of security.

A second curricular model could be called the social exchange or "contract model." The operative term in the contract model is that of negotiation. In this curricular type, students negotiate a more or less individualized program. In practice, the contract model takes two different forms. These are here called the "closed contract" model and the "open contract" model. The closed contract is distinguished by its constriction of the process of negotiation. The period of negotiation occurs prior to the formalization of a contract. Renegotiation occurs only with the consent of faculty and usually follows recognition of a problem in the original contract. Faculty see many student requests for renegotiation as evidence of student failures to live up to performance requirements agreed upon in the contract. The real difference between the closed contract model and the performance model is the recognition of student differences in the closed contract model. Programs which view the student as signing a contract by matriculating into a prepackaged program are really performance models. With the closed contract model, the student generates individualized curriculum packages subject to faculty approval. In most places, this involves a liberal selection of courses by the student with individual study filling in the gaps. The burden of proof is on the student to demonstrate a coherence behind his choices, and in many instances this involves a performance test at the culmination of the program.

In the closed contract model, students usually have discretion to select faculty advisors and subject matter concentration. In the process of negotiation leading to a contract, the student must consider his learning objectives and select methods of accomplishing them. The extent to which faculty guide and direct student choices is variable. Faculty approve student programs with reference to the implicit or explicit expectations within their particular college or department. In this way, the relationships of authority between college, faculty, and students prevail.

The closed contract curriculum may be analogous to the transition between conformist and conscientious stages mentioned by Loevinger. This transition is called the self-conscious stage. What Loevinger calls proto-complexity (emerging awareness of multiplicity or relativity) is represented in the closed contract curriculum by the circumscribed choices students are permitted. The push for individuality arising from awakening consciousness of inner feelings is appeased by the offering of quasi-individualized education. Meanwhile, the needs for reassurance typical of the earlier stage of conformity are maintained in curricular structuring. Thus, the contradictions of the closed contract curriculum match the inner conflicts of the self-conscious stage.

The open contract model is differentiated from the closed contract model by removal of constrictions from the process of negotiation, and by acknowledgement of the validity of individual goalsetting. The open contract model assumes that individualized learning is a continuing process requiring sustained student initiative. This is in contrast to the static nature of negotiation embodied in the closed contract. Reciprocity in faculty-student relationships is basic to the open contract model. The expectation for students is that they will take initiative in developing their learning programs. This includes the continuous consideration of learning goals and activities as well as the development of methods of evaluation. Parameters are placed on student choices. Faculty authority is generally asserted when students fail to present evidence of self-defined learning activities. Faculty challenge students to examine the changing relationships between their activities and goals.

The open contract model is analogous to the conscientious or social contract stages formulated by Loevinger and Kohlberg respectively. The conscientious person is self-critical, strives for goals, is aware of choices, is concerned with improving himself, and achievement is important and is measured by one's own inner standards. Kohlberg describes this level as reflecting a concern for maintaining the respect of others, and seeing duty as defined in terms of contract. The criticism of potential malingering appropriate for lower stages is clearly inapplicable for this stage, since persons at this stage are preoccupied with questions of priorities. Conformity at this stage is not to rules or established structures, but to shared or shareable rights and duties. At its best, professionalism typifies this stage. For example, professions strive to achieve subcultures which are characterized by reciprocal relationships, shared standards of excellence and ethics, and altruistic responsibilities.

Strengths of the open contract model are that it (1) demands student initiative, (2) individualizes learning relevant to student interests and needs, (3) capitalizes on student motivation to learn, (4) requires student-faculty dialogue, (5) allows students the flexibility to schedule and determine the duration of learning activities, and (6) catalyzes student self-evaluation. In addition, the open contract model accommodates institutional and professional demands. It permits certification of students and satisfies demands for faculty control. Although more pluralistic than performance and closed contract models, open contract models tend to use similar criteria to measure success.

The open contract model suffers from a number of weaknesses. Faculty-student relationships are covertly based on authority as contrasted with aforementioned models which are manifestly authoritarian. Students have responsibility but no formal power. The burden of proof as to the soundness and quality of program rests with the student, but certification power rests with the faculty. At worst, faculty exercise authority in the manner of the closed contract model. At best, faculty authority is benevolently exercised. The attempt is to produce independence through paternalism. This is a contradiction many parents have painfully confronted. There is an ever-present potential for deceit in which students face contradictory demands. The overt message is to demand independence while the covert message is to expect emulation of faculty models. The open contract model can place onerous psychological stress on students. This is particularly true for students who need to live up to internal standards (which are frequently hypercritical) and to obtain faculty recognition. Under such circumstances, the open contract model tends to accentuate any existing student tendencies toward anxiety, insecurity and competition with self and others. Insecurity tends to drive students to seek relief through performance, which detracts from questioning, experimentation, and acceptance of self. This is a poor style of learning, especially for those preparing to become human service professionals. The need to help may become so great that students will later repeat the paternalistic style in working with clients.

The openness of the contract model is partially a function of (1) faculty pluralism, (2) the stages of ego development of individual faculty members (and of students), (3) the extent to which faculty and administrators tolerate ambiguity. Along with faculty characteristics, important factors in determining the openness of a contract curriculum are the rules under which a program operates and the rigidity and specificity with which the program is monitored by institutional, departmental, or external agencies.

The fourth conceptual model is that of the "experimenting community" (cf. Bilorusky, 1972), where learning experiences emerge from a process of interaction. This interaction may involve students, faculty and other professionals, and community people. This model is seen as corresponding with Loevinger's autonomous stage and Kohlberg's stage of conscience or principle orientation. Loevinger states that this stage is so named partly because one recognizes other people's need for autonomy and partly because individuals are more free of excessive striving and feelings of responsibility. There is concern with social problems beyond the scope of the person's immediate experience, and there is an attempt to be objective and realistic about self and others. Kohlberg describes persons at this stage as being oriented to conscience as a directing agent and to mutual respect and trust. The autonomous person experiments in his continuing search for self-fulfillment, understanding, and justice. Respect for the autonomy of others allows possibilities for collaboration not likely in lower stages, although it is recognized that such interaction can occur in other models.

The experimenting community differs from other curricular models in its approach to education as well as in its epistemology. Rather than separating science and social action, the experimenting community is based on a methodology which integrates thinking and acting (cf. Glaser and Strauss, 1967; Blumer, 1969). Members of experimenting communities are necessarily aware of the unity of the process of learning and that which is being learned. This approach can be contrasted with traditional methods of science (cf. Carnap, 1966) and of professional practice in the human services (cf. Thomas, 1967 pp. 38-48).

T. S. Kuhn (1961) has provided us with an understanding of the way disciplines maintain continuity through educational techniques in which students learn paradigms by studying exemplars of the paradigms. By solving problems defined by a traditional paradigm, students learn the paradigm without ever needing to examine the fundamental assumptions or tenets of the paradigm. In this respect, the student becomes a mere puzzle-solver. When a science reaches the stage of puzzle-solving, it has been transformed from science (the context of discovery and experimentation) to technology. If the student encounters a circumstance alien to his paradigm, it is either not perceived, or it is explained in paradigmatic terms which might appear implausible to a more critical observer. To the professional practitioner trapped within his orthodoxy, the implausible is not questioned. In fact, the expedient advantage of paradigms is that a practitioner need not bother himself with so many questions, and he can be about his work with a degree of certainty. This is satisfactory so long as the problems fit the technology. Potential harm is possible when technologies are blindly applied to problems for which they were never intended. Psychoanalytic theory and behavior modification are examples of practice theories in the human service professions which are treated as paradigms by their proponents. Practitioners of the former learn from case histories and case consultations, while practitioners of the latter learn from experiments reported in the literature. In either case, learning is by exemplar and is constricted by problem definitions dictated by the respective paradigms.

By contrast, the nature of the experimenting community is probably best captured by the concept of "script improvisation." The learning process involves a continuing dialectic between script and improvisation. This method avoids learning by exemplar and the rigidities of paradigms. Script improvisation has direct implications for connecting theory and action, since such distinctions are not inherent in the learning process. The experimenting community differs from mere experience-learning in which individuals, believing they are operating without theory, may impose implicit personal theories or scripts on the world. In fact, this is the pitfall which theories are supposed to overcome. Theories and scripts bring their own pitfalls of reification and overgeneralization. By participating in the dialectic of script improvisation, individuals learn the process of interaction between theory and action. By continuously examining and constructing scripts and theories in an action context, distortions become apparent. A parallel research methodology may be found in the works of Blumer (1969) and of Glaser and Strauss (1967).

The experimenting community embodies continuous self-examination and self-confrontation, and in so doing, its participants avoid the subjectivity of unrecognized personal scripts or entrapment into paradigms. For those operating under the constraints of a paradigm, script improvision is difficult to effect or understand. Faculty must be tolerant of ambiguity if they are to recognize that student ideas are not exemplars of faculty paradigms, but may have very different meanings for students. The learning schemas of faculty have been more performance oriented, and it is always tempting to straighten out students when they wander into what seems to be fruitless exploration. By paradigmatic interpretation of student ideas and actions, faculty defiine the learning situation. This is a dynamic of the hidden curriculum not present in the experimenting community. The faculty role is that of calling attention to and recognizing the value of script improvisation. In fact, students often help faculty recognize their own potential for improvisational learning. Collegiality emerges from such understanding, assistance, and challenge.

The above conceptual framework emerged largely out of the authors' experiences in developing the ILP. The research methodology used by the authors was similar to the process of script improvisation described in the previous several pages. Concepts were developed by participant-observation in an action context. The authors sought exemplars and anomalies for emerging concepts; these exemplars and anomalies to concepts came from the authors' experiences with the ILP. In presenting concepts, principles and strategies in this article, the authors will use examples from the ILP to illustrate and clarify the concepts and strategies. However, the length of this article does not permit a presentation of the full scope and detail of the evidence which led to the development of the concepts discussed in this article. Here, the authors are not concerned with proving and demonstrating the validity of this conceptual framework, but rather with providing others with a theoretical perspective which they may use, test, modify, and in some cases, reject or verify.

IMPROVISATIONAL LEARNING

One of the essential features of an experimenting community is that it helps individuals to critically and openly explore and examine their relations with the world. Through a critical, searching, and holistic perspective, an individual creates his own scripts of thought and action. The individual asserts himself, making choices and becoming more autonomous. Instead of being bound by the scripts created by others, the individual improvises from existing scripts and is involved in a continuing process of creating his own scripts. A major challenge for faculty (and students) in creating a curriculum which is based on the model of the experimenting community (in part at least) is to collaboratively create a program script (or learning context) of script improvisation.

The process of script improvisation is person-centered, not contract-centered. With improvisational learning, the starting point from which one departs is not ultimately important, whereas the direction and process of subsequent growth is crucial. This growth is necessarily open-ended and always unfolding, but toward greater autonomy and toward a heightened commitment and sensitivity to social justice. Indeed, students in the ILP have many different scripts—different concerns, interests, and values. To some, the acceptance of all student scripts as valid starting points for the process of script improvisation may seem like amoral pluralism, permissiveness, or plain indifference. In an experimenting community, such diversity is affirmed, because of a respect for the fundamental dignity and autonomy of all individuals and because of the potential for growth represented by each individual regardless of his "starting point."

Developmental Themes

A few comments about some of the themes of student development observed in the ILP may help to clarify several aspects of improvisational learning. Most students began to ask more questions of themselves—about their learning directions, about their commitments, about the human service professions, and about the larger society. Students became more concerned with the importance of developing a personal philosophy. Most students became more sensitive to the fact that there are different assumptions and values underlying different definitions of problems. It is not obvious how one goes about identifying community problems. During the year, students in the ILP became less likely to see community services as a technology of how to solve obvious and objectively existing problems. Because ILP students had to organize their experiences, they eventually had to construct a personal approach to the identification of problems. They could not rely on faculty or agency supervisors or on course outlines to provide them with problem definitions.

It appeared to the authors that, increasingly, students asked themselves ethical questions—what are my responsibilities to society as a whole and to my clients as individuals? What values should inform my selection of community involvements? And, they raised aesthetic questions more frequently—what constitutes beauty and joy in life? What would a beautiful society be like? What would a society be like if it gave everyone maximum opportunities to pursue their own notions of "good" and "beautiful"? Students became especially concerned with epistemological questions. How do I know that I know? What constitutes real learning? How can I develop better, more critical and more open, methods of learning and knowing?

However, immobilization and hyperactivity both represented a phase of transition into the new program, where external authority and rigid contracts were minimized and where script improvisation was actively encouraged. These two seemingly different responses to the situation were usually followed or accompanied by a period of self-examination. Many students were immobilized by the unstructured qualities of the program. They often did not have classes or any pre-set schedules to follow. So, they had to decide for themselves how to spend their time. In many cases, it took students several weeks (to several months, in a few cases) before they were taking initiative in making decisions about their lives. Other students worked fast and furiously at the beginning, piling up paper after paper as a means of self-assurance, without really searching for the personal relevance in their learning activties.

One important learning experience for many students in the ILP was to discover that the Individualized Learning Program cannot be "THE answer." Alternatives and freedom cannot be given to students by faculty. But through the collaborative process, faculty could confront students with the possibility of their actively participating in creating their own alternatives and freedom. Students were confronted with an awareness that learning is not limited to certain hours of day, days of week, or weeks of year. Everything is a potential learning experience. As one student commented, "it's a hard thing to get used to." Moreover, most students expressed the view that it takes time to understand the concepts underlying an experimenting community.

Some faculty have argued that students should make the transition from the regular curriculum to the ILP by first performing well in courses or independent study. The authors feel that this does not really constitute a transition. Total immersion in the climate of the experimenting community seems necessary to produce the type of introspection which leads to script improvisation. One unique and essential aspect of the ILP was that the student had to confront the issue of how to plan, create, and select his learning experiences. So long as he is involved in regular courses, he will tend to be dependent on that structure—at least until he passes through a kind of crisis period of trying to decide how to determine his own learning experiences. This is why one of the authors questioned students about their enrolling in courses. At other universities, it has been observed that when students take some structured courses with independent study or more unstrucured, student-directed courses, the structure of the regular courses often places demands on students which deflect their attention from the self-directing possibilities in the unstructured settings.

Even the contract-centered curriculum can be detracting from the continued self-examination needed for the development of autonomy and improvisational learning. Contracts often force or seduce students into becoming fixed on their initial goals. For example, if one student would have used his initial goal of wanting to be a juvenille probation officer as an unquestioned basis for subsequent learning, he may never have discovered the larger context toward which his initial goal was directed, community education. If contractually stated goals become the principal guide for learning, students will then be unnecessarily limited by their past experiences and by those societal roles which are most common and highly sanctioned or publicized in the status quo. People are often limited by their conceptions of available life alternatives or roles. One of the purposes of improvisational learning is to encourage people to explore and create new alternatives and directions for themselves.

For most students, by the midpoint of the academic year, the concern with self-examination had widened to include intense engagement with theory development and community action. Increasingly, the learning activities of students revealed emerging syntheses of "personal" and "professional" activities, values, concepts, and commitments. Some of the most salient features of individual development in curricular models based on contract and improvisational learning may be summarized as follows. Student commitments, within contract models, are at worst made to fixed, concrete goals; at best they are made to changeable and more general goals. In the context of script improvisation, a person's commitments are to a general direction; the commitment emanates from the script presented and moves toward the future with the openness of improvisation. Commitment and change are unified in the process of improvisational learning. The open contract model, without the influence of the experimenting community, permits both commitment and change without stimulating an effort to integrate the two.

Community Experience

In the regular curricula, field studies often provide a context where students are passively socialized into the scripts of established agencies. Just as students may uncritically accept the theories of faculty, so may they unconsciously and uncritically learn the paradigms of professional practice used by their agency supervisors and coworkers. In the ILP, field placements were developed through student initiative rather than as part of a package of learning modules (e. g., courses). It was up to the ILP student to contact the agency and work out a contract for a working/learning relationship with them. Since ILP students took the initiative in developing their placements, they found themselves from the outset in a more collaborative relationship with agency people. Some faculty were surprised at the collegial relationships students were able to develop with agency people, who, in the context of the regular curriculum, would have been inclined to assume positions of authority with respect to students.

The ILP also allowed students an important flexibility in scheduling their commuity involvement activities, for they were not required to fit these activities within a highly constricting course schedule. In some cases, this helped ILP students to find jobs in the field of community services—they were then able to support themselves and at the same time be involved in a highly stimulating learning situation. In addition, students could negotiate the duration and extent of each community involvement in light of changing developments, with respect to both the student's learning needs and the agency. If a student wished, he could have more than one placement for some period of time; and at other times, he could choose to focus on organizing his past experiences and on exploring new theories without being involved in the community.

In general, ILP student field experiences were individualized and varied. Students sought out experiences ranging from merely visiting agencies and talking with staff to participating as observers or volunteers. Many students participated simultaneously at several agencies. With faculty assistance, students used agency opportunities to highlight the learning of ideas, to find examples of theories, to identify and understand problems, and to develop practice skills. Moreover, community experiences helped students to acquaint themselves with the kinds of services available in selected fields, and to critically compare and evaluate these services.

No agency complained about the participation of ILP students and many offered positive comments. The usual complaints about field placement, the usual series of meetings to discuss interagency problems about sharing a student did not occur. It is likely that many of these meetings arise out of a need to control students in the usual field placement setup. There is no reason to believe that students learned any less from self-initiated, self-administered field placements than from contrived, controlled, and structured field placements.

Indeed, the absence of formal structure and the stimulation provided by interaction with faculty encouraged students to confront the problem of integrating theory and action. It seems that student initiative in selecting and defining field placements encourages a better use of concurrent life experiences (including theoretical readings)—the student comes to be very conscious of the sense in which all experiences are potentially learning experiences and of the possibilities for interrelating these experiences. Because no one else is organizing the student's experiences for him, as is done implicitly by the way courses are organized, the student has to actively confront the issue of how to organize and make sense out of his experiences.

In some curricula, on the other hand, there is an attempt to integrate theory and action through field placement seminars. However, this is another example of a modular, nonimprovisational, approach to learning. It is contrived; it is an attempt to effect a linkage of curricular structures—the theoretical structures of classes and the action structures of field placements. It is not person-centered but structure-centered, or module-centered. Such seminars do not create situations where the integration of experiences must come from the individual. In some ways, they may serve as crutches which detract the individual's attention from the continuing importance of integrating theory and action, whether one is in the classroom or in the community.

Most models of learning are further constrained by the fact that many field instructors and faculty believe that students must learn certain scripts of professional practice *before* they become capable of pursuing independent study. This view of learning fits in with the ideas of pre-packaged and competency-based education, where it is assumed that the areas of relevant knowledge are rather obvious and well-defined. This assumption is subject to serious question in any field of study and professional practice, but especially so in the human service professions (cf. Kuhn, 1962).

By contrast, improvisational learning represents a situation where students learn different scripts *while* they are learning the process of script improvisation. The learning of different views, theories, techniques, and methods outlined by others is part, but only part, of a total process of learning where students actively participate in the development of scripts. Script development and script improvisation thus becomes a living process in which the student is immersed; the student is not merely exposed to the professionally legitimized products of someone else's process of script development.

In most curricula, students are said to have a "breadth" of knowledge when they have acquired familiarity with a number of accepted faculty scripts (or theories). The relationships among these scripts and between these scripts and various aspects of the "real world" are either ignored, or else the relationships are taught to students as predefined and static realities. Students have no opportunities to explore and discover such relationships for themselves, in the context of the living process of script development.

In the context of improvisational learning, then, students are more likely to develop a holistic approach to their experiences. For example, in the ILP, there was a strong tendency for students to become aware of different levels of analysis rather than to be confined by a few theories or the routine practices of agencies. For example, one student simultaneously considered both the effects of child care practices on individual development and the relations between the politics of women's liberation and the child care movement. The student developed an emerging awareness of the relationships between various levels of analysis, between what some people refer to as the macro- and micro-levels of analysis.

CONFRONTING LEARNING-CERTIFICATION CONTRADICTIONS

Because colleges award degrees to students, aspects of either the performance model or the contract model are incorporated into all curricula. In many ways, the principles of the experimenting community and of improvisational learning are antithetical to the certification of students.

The contradictions between learning and certification are strongly reflected in the processes of student evaluation. In many individualized learning programs, such as the ILP, each student prepares a file of evidence of learning or a learning portfolio. Such files are in some respects analogous to artists' portfolios, except in some programs, students are concerned with articulating the processes as well as the products of their learning. The files often include papers, project descriptions, self-evaluations, personal diaries, evaluations by faculty, students, and members of the larger community, as well as any other data which give insight into a student's learning experiences.

To the extent that such files are viewed as products for assessing student competency and for making certification decisions, to that extent the contract model is emphasized. To the extent that the files are seen as a way of facilitating learning and as part of a continuing process of script improvisation, to that extent the idea of the "experimenting community" is emphasized. The relative emphases placed on certification and learning are expressed in the contrasts of the *product view* and the *heuristic view* of the learning portfolios.

The centrality of the certification function in institutions of higher education (cf. Illich, 1971; Jencks and Riesman, 1968) supports and encourages the product view of the learning file. For example, many students in the ILP experienced a kind of "anticipatory inhibition." The very fact that students were required to develop a file of evidence of learning helped give rise to student fears that their academic work might be too far out for their advisors. And, many students who were highly involved in the learning process were sometimes annoyed by the distraction of having to package their personally meaningful learning experiences in terms which would be understandable to "academic accounters." For example, one student expressed the view that "the file conveys a hidden curriculum . . . (it seems to imply) this is the cost of being in the program (the ILP), for which you should be grateful."

At the same time, the learning file can have an important heuristic value. In developing the file, the student must struggle with the question of what criteria and data to use in self-evaluation—as a learner and as an apprentice professional. Students in the ILP learned that it is certainly not obvious what values and standards should be applied to human service professionals (or to any other professional area) as they join with others in creating a more humane society. The file of evidence of learning can encourage the exploration of such value questions as what is "professionally competent," "personally meaningful," and "socially just"? The file can provide the student with a context in which to improve his understanding of his strengths and weaknesses. Through the file, the student can portray the ways he has struggled with the problems, conflicts, and dilemmas involved in his learning process and in his actions towards others.

In large part, the heuristic view of learning files assumes that by articulating one's experiences to others, one can obtain better insight into the meaning of those experiences and into their relations to other experiences and arenas of activity. For example, one student was able to gain much insight into the limitations of a social agency with which she had been working for a number of years because the ILP encouraged her to articulate the strengths and weaknesses of her professional practices. But other students have sometimes found little value in communicating their experiences to others, except through informal conversations. The limitations on the heuristic value of a semi-formalized communication of one's learning experiences to others remain uncertain. Maybe such formalized articulations are not that helpful to all people? Indeed, one might ask, do all faculty who advocate the heuristic view of learning portfolios keep such portfolios for themselves? Or perhaps files facilitate learning only in certain situations and at certain times At times, writing things down for the file of evidence can help the student to learn it; at other times, the student can become so busy documenting his learning activities for the file, that he no longer takes time to ask himself questions about the personal and social relevance of his learning activities.

A continuing challenge for faculty and students engaged in improvisational learning is to distinguish between authentic translation, amplification, and communication of learning experiences and contrived representations of learning for purposes of accountability. These two perspectives can be referred to as the previously mentioned "heuristic" and "product" views of learning files. If the student feels the file is primarily viewed by faculty as a means for certifying learning, then even potentially meaningful articulations of learning experiences may come to seem contrived. In such situations, the file of evidence of learning can be merely the means by which students demonstrate to faculty that they have "lived up" to their contracts.

The student's file is most likely to facilitate learning when it is in the context of collegial relations with faculty. Learning files can become bases for collaboration and dialogue on the student's learning activities and on issues and activities of mutual importance to student and advisors. However, even when there is student-faculty collaboration, the fact that the file is a *requirement* for certification may convey the subtle but strong message that the file is a product to be judged.

Faculty and students who wish to move toward genuine participation in collaborative and improvisational learning must acknowledge rather than deny such contradictions between learning and certification. For example, the file of evidence of learning should be viewed as a double-edged sword. The file can help students (and faculty) to examine their learning over a period of time—they can use it to see how they have changed. It can be a context for organizing ideas, for conceptualizing experiences, for directing subsequent action, and generally for integrating theory and action. On the other hand, it can detract from learning if it comes to be the end and goal of learning rather than part of a very extensive process. Maybe the metaphors of "file" or "portfolio" overemphasize the product view. A file seems to suggest a temporally and spatially closed area into which one files pieces of one's experiences. Indeed, part of the seductive appeal of the file, as an instrument of certification and public documentation, is that it has the appearance of permanence. But in fact, it dies when it is viewed as permanent—slices of experience are removed from the stream of time and reified. The heuristic view, by contrast, suggests that learning porfolios can be used in integrating past, present, and future experiences. They can provide starting points for oneself and others as invitations and introductions to personal and shared learning. A file can serve as an edge on the fabric of learning, or as some way into the fabric.

One way of exploring further the influence of certification on open curricula is to examine the minimum standards for the awarding of credit and a degree. The minimal qualifications for certification of students in the ILP are interesting because they represent one fusion of the open contract model and the concept of improvisational learning, basic to an experimenting community. Could a student remain in the ILP and receive credit if he was doing "too little" learning or the "wrong" kinds of learning? And, who should participate in the asking and answering of such questions? Three general guidelines for certifying student engagement in the learning process were typically used in the ILP.

First, the student was expected to take initiative and primary responsibility for directing his learning. This meant that the student should be struggling with his learning directions, activities, and self-evaluation without continual prodding from the faculty advisors. The student may ask advisors for assistance and support, and would be encouraged to do so, but he was expected to increasingly take the lead in directing his learning. The sensitive application of this guideline involves some interesting problems. For example, are students breaking this part of the contract if they fail to take initiative after two months? It took most students a considerable period to pass through a transition crisis of adjusting to the reality of self-directed learning. Certainly, it is to be expected that some students will take longer than others, especially if one attempts to make such programs accessible to more than a very select group of highly autonomous and self-motivated students. But how long? What kind of progress and/or struggle with the crisis of transition should be expected at the minimum? And who should decide whether or not the students are in fact taking initiative?

The decision-making process for such circumstances in the ILP was as follows. Any faculty member could withdraw from a student's advisory committee at any time, if he felt the student was not making "sufficient progress" (in becoming more independent). The student then had several options—return to the regular program (after receiving full credit for his ILP work); get another faculty member to replace the advisor who withdrew; or, if he felt the faculty member had acted capriciously he could appeal the matter to the College's ethics and standards committee. In fact, several students were issued "ultimatums" by faculty but they usually rose to the occasion and began to take more initiative in their learning (albeit in response to the faculty member's challenge).

This general process was designed not only to provide a fairly just approach to certification, but also to facilitate the development of student autonomy and improvisational learning. By allowing students to select their advisors, the diversity of student interests and needs was accommodated. Consequently, after a period of exploration, students and faculty were able to establish working relations with those individuals with whom they could best collaborate. Indeed the successful confrontation of student motivation and mobilization problems often depended on the willingness of a faculty member to commit himself to the collegial process with the student. Because most decision-making and responsibility for the learning process was decentralized to the level of the student and his advisors, this made the certification and learning processes potentially more pluralistic and personcentered.

A second, related minimum guideline was that the student must show how his learning had personal relevance. Students articulated the significance and importance of their learning activities instead of merely relying on external criteria for validation of their learning. An example of this principle can be seen in the way one of the authors interacted with students who wanted to enroll in a regular course. He did not tell them they could not do it, but he asked them many questions: Why can't you learn the same things without taking a course? Why don't you sit in on the lectures and/ or discussions, but don't formally enroll in the course? Why don't you formulate your own assignments instead of placing yourself in a situation where you will follow the professor's assignments? Why don't you develop your own syllabus for the course, perhaps using the professor's as a script for improvisation? The authors' hypothesize that after the student has had the solid experience of continuously and consistently asking himself such questions for a year or so, then he will always do it; and to a large extent, he can enroll in classes in the future (e. g., in graduate school) without being dependent on the external authority of professors or on the preestablished structures of classes.

The third guideline resulted from the fact that the ILP was in the College of Community Services. Faculty felt that much of the student's learning should be relevant to the general area of community services. At the same time, it was recognized that the definition and limits of the field of community services, and indeed of all fields, are necessarily open and in process. Students were encouraged and expected to develop and articulate their own conceptions of "community services," and to use these conceptions as a basis for many of their learning experiences (i. e., as scripts for improvisation).

COLLABORATIVE ADVISING

In programs, such as the ILP, which combine aspects of the open contract model with the aspects of the experimenting community, student-faculty relations have a dual quality. Faculty are negotiating with the students in the continual formulation and reformulation of open-ended and changing learning directions (open contracts), and they are also collaborating with each other in a process of improvisational learning. From the standpoint of a faculty member's perspective, this dual quality of student-faculty relationships may be described as "collaborative advising" for person-centered, improvisational learning. This approach to advising can be contrasted to two increasingly popular forms of individualized advising—the competency-based approach to advising and the so-called "nondirective" approach.

In collaborative advising, faculty challenge students to grow, to become autonomous, to become sensitive to ethical issues, to become aware of different scripts, and to develop the ability to improvise. With the competency-based approach, students are expected to learn the professionally appropriate (i. e., commonly accepted) skills, values, and theories. This latter approach envisions society as a "professionalized meritocracy." Faculty see students in terms of what they do rather than what they are. With the person-centered approach, faculty help and challenge students to develop those qualities of autonomous personhood which will enable students to identify and develop those competencies which they see as most relevant to themselves and mankind.

However, the person-centered approach can be misinterpreted and abused. Faculty may use their authority to reify and define student experience and identity. In this way, learning becomes "rehabilitation" and colleges support tendencies toward a "therapeutic state" (cf. Kittrie, 1971). Often faculty and students alike are unaware of the subtle ways in which faculty use their authority to define and direct student experience—this is especially true of those strategies of advising and counseling which are referred to as "nondirective."

With the competency-based approach, the emphasis is on the student *coping* with the tasks of setting goals, implementing activities which achieve those goals, and demonstrating his professionally-defined competencies. The learning process is constricted because the student is held accountable for the effectiveness with which he enters into the process *as it is conceptualized by the faculty member*. With collaborative advising, the faculty member challenges the student to articulate open-ended learning directions rather than specific learning goals. He encourages students to define and clarify their learning directions by exploring the larger personal and social contexts in which they are embedded. Student learning activities are then guided more by holistic patterns or networks of concerns and arenas of involvement than by concrete objectives. Moreover, the faculty member is likely to confront the student with the dilemmas and difficulties involved in assessing his own competencies and learning activities. For example, he may suggest that the student view his criteria for evaluating learning as in a state of flux, and as emerging from the very process of learning itself.

One question many students ask themselves and their advisors is—how much of my advisor's judgments and suggestions do I accept? Faculty sometimes respond to this questioning by attempting to become nondirective facilitators. They strive to be nonassertive, believing that if they reveal nothing of their own views, there will be nothing for students to accept. Usually, however, such approaches result in subtle communications to the student of what is acceptable. And, because of the subtle, covert character of this process, students and faculty are unlikely to recognize and deal with the manipulation and conformity which may thwart the development of student autonomy and script improvisation. In attempting to develop a more collaborative approach to advising, the authors would often challenge student scripts, support attempts at improvisation, suggest alternative scripts and arenas of exploration (all of these activities being quite "directive"). At the same time, students were encouraged to be openly critical of our ideas.

The challenges of collaborative advising are indeed very difficult as well as personally involving and satisfying. Faculty must give students support and encouragement as well as straightforward and honest criticism. Faculty must remove themselves from the subtle paternalism found in the nondirective approach and instead authentically pose problems, suggest directions, and express personal commitments and beliefs. At the same time, faculty must not allow students to think such statements necessarily represent the best formulations of problems, the most actualizing and humane directions, or the most moral and informed commitments. The creative synthesis of these qualities poses a strong challenge to faculty, not only in terms of their relationships with students, but with respect to their relations with each other and with persons from the larger community, for these qualities are at the heart of the collaborative process and the collective side of the learning process.

Indeed, individualized learning programs based on collaboration, a quest for justice, person-centered relations, and improvisational learning have important liberating possibilities for faculty. One of the frustrating and constricting aspects of teaching can be found in the way students sometimes reify faculty views and opinions into "absolute" truths; this tendency is encouraged by the meta-messages of closed curricula. In performance curricula and competency-based models, faculty are more easily forced into a position of nondirective selflessness and amorality, if they attempt to prevent students from uncritically adopting their views. On the other hand, when curricula explicitly deemphasize faculty authority and explicitly expect student autonomy and initiative, faculty are freer to express their views and commitments to students. The meta-messages of these more open curricula discourage students from uncritically accepting faculty views or misinterpreting faculty statements as a "party-line" to follow in making the grade. In the ILP, for example, it was generally expected that people would openly express their commitments and views, that others would listen to them, and that others would not uncritically accept these positions.

Since the success of open and person-centered curricula is especially dependent upon the openness of the involved faculty, faculty development takes on a special importance. Noonan (1972, pp. 191-201) has suggested that the development of faculty teaching abilities is best facilitated by immersing faculty in innovative curricula, rather than by merely presenting research reports and workshops to faculty. The authors' observations support this view. In the ILP, most faculty learning, like student learning, involved immersion for an extended period in the processes of improvisational learning and collaboration. The role of the educational change agent is therefore similar to the approach of collaborative advising described above. The change agent encourages faculty participation in a curriculum aimed toward improvisational learning, and he participates with faculty in the innovative curriculum. Together, they confront the problems involved in teaching and learning in this new setting. This is in contrast to the low-key process consultant who works with faculty for only brief periods and who focuses on the problems faculty encounter in traditional curricula.

THE LARGER IMPLICATIONS OF EXPERIMENTING COMMUNITIES

The experimenting community represents certain patterns of collective activity and nurtures certain processes of learning and change (e. g., the development of individual autonomy, a committed quest for social justice, and improvisational learning). These processes are expressions of the openness and intentions of the individuals involved, and, at the same time, they can be supported or hindered by different patterns of collective activity which may enchance or oppose the intentions of the individuals involved.

On the one hand, the creation of experimenting communities is in the hands of the persons involved. Principles such as the ones discussed in this article may be reified and made into standard procedures (rules) or into constricted, closed contracts. Openness and a commitment to experimentation on the part of individual faculty and students is important in preventing what seems to be the natural tendency for social organizations to move in the direction of conformity to rules and consensual norms. On the other hand, the openness and genuine intentions of individual students and faculty to encourage improvisational learning may be thwarted by closed curricular structures. The different curricular models tend to exert important (if sometimes subtle) pressures toward different types of human development, social change, and professional practice. It is important, therefore, to examine the different visions of man and society implied by these models.

The frames of reference for evaluating action and learning in experimenting communities are both personal and holistic—they are based on a respect for the autonomy of the individuals involved and on a concern with the meaning of personal activities for mankind or society as a whole. The ethics which are reflected in the interaction and collective action of experimenting communities have both more personal and more universal groundings than the ethics of established organizations. Contracts, roles, organizational norms, established authority are all subordinate to the respect for individual autonomy and to the concern for mankind and social justice. By contrast, learning and action in contract curricula are typically evaluated in light of professional and institutional definitions of "competency." Institutional and professional authority and/or consensus define the limits and the desired directions for learning activities.

The contract curricula are consistent with a view of man as "modular man." Human development is seen as a modular system where the individual directs his growth by putting together an individaulized set of "personality packages." Life in the modular world is primarily a matter of selecting from among preexisting modules (e. g., roles) over which one has little or no control. Individuals cannot create or modify the modules which make up the social fabric.

The experimenting community, by contrast, assumes that it is possible for individuals to create their own roles and social relations quite beyond the constraints of preexisting social definitions and roles. Individuals create meaning and purposes, and their relations and roles reflect these purposes, rather than the opposite as is the assumption of contract settings. Personal identity need not be limited by the constraints of social modules, for the individual can be a central and creative agent in his own developmental processes.

The contract model of education allows students to adapt to the future, so that students can move beyond the traditional assumptions and roles implied by the performance model with its prepackaged courses. The contract model of education is often justified by the argument that to live in a rapidly changing society, people must learn how to actively adapt to changing environmental conditions. Moreover, in such a society, many contemporary professions will lose their identity and merge with other professions; professional roles will rapidly change, and many decisions will be made by task forces of professionals which will be constituted on an ad hoc basis (cf. Toffler, 1970; Bennis and Slater, 1968). The performance curriculum does not prepare people for such ready adaptability. But the contract model does. It encourages the individual to actively participate in the process of planning his learning and living so that he can "fit into" the emerging society of the future.

By contrast, improvisational learning and the experimenting community aim to enable the individual to create the society of the future rather than to merely adapt to it. External criteria such as contracts, anticipated societal developments, roles, changing professional norms or demands are not the major frames of reference for the experimenting community. Instead, the person-in-the-world becomes the focus for learning and living. It is concerned with persons and with a quest for universal principles of justice rather than with tasks, roles, and statuses; and it is a process grounded in commitment as well as experimentation, rather than a closed commitment to goals or an uncommitted search for direction. It is in and through this holistic process of improvisational growth and experience that the autonomy of the individual emerges.

Even in light of its humanistic assumptions, one might ask whether the experimenting community is the best curriculum for all students. Indeed, one question often asked by faculty participants and observers of the ILP was, "who belongs in the ILP"? Some believed that the regular curriculum would be best suited for those students who need structure, while the ILP would be appropriate for the more independent and highly self-motivated students. A few even expressed the view that the ILP would be best for those students with distinguished records of performance in the traditional program. Others maintained that the program should meet the demands of mass higher education by serving all kinds of students. The advocates of elitism feared that most students are incapable of self-direction, while the proponents of a pluralistic student population feared exclusiveness and possible social inequities from concentrating academic resources on a fortunate few. An assumption of the experimenting community is that all students can grow and benefit from improvisational learning.

To some extent, constraints on faculty time available to the ILP compromised the principles of pluralistic participation. Faculty time is most extensively used by students who are not highly self-motivated, because much interaction is usually necessary to help such students make the transition to open curricula. Realizing this, many faculty in the ILP made little effort to encourage students who are not highly independent and self-motivated to enter the ILP. However, such programs might free up faculty time by obtaining grant monies for extra faculty, by reducing the proliferation of courses in the regular program, and eventually, by increased reliance on students who have developed a high degree of autonomy and who understand the subtleties and complexities of learning in an experimenting community. After an initially high investment of faculty time for a year or two in the development of students in the experimenting community, these students would be highly independent learners who would place relatively few demands on faculty time and who could be highly helpful to other students.

Perhaps the most crucial challenge for faculty participating in open curricula is to help students with a mediocre degree of autonomy and self-motivation to develop into autonomous and self-directing learners. Therefore, one of the biggest problems facing faculty is not the problem of selecting students who are most likely to "make it" in the program, but rather to encourage students with a variety of personal qualities and backgrounds to participate in open curricula and to help them make the difficult transition from traditional learning situations.

10 NEAL R BERTE

The Future for
Learning Contracts

It should be obvious from the previous case studies of present-day approaches to learning contracts that contracting implements many of the concepts usually included in any definition of nontraditional study—that learning is not bound by time or place, that what students know is more important than how they have gained that knowledge, that new clientele should be served by higher education, that each student should be treated as an individual with distinctive educational and vocational needs, that faculty and staff should serve as mentors and learning facilitators for students, that curricula should move away from the pattern of separate and isolated disciplinary offerings to interdisciplinary approaches, and that degrees should be awarded on the basis of conpetence rather than the accumulation of a magic number of credits.*

It should be equally obvious that the approaches to contracting are many and varied. Thus far *contracting* in higher education has come to mean any of three categories of plans: (1) contracting for grades, (2) contracting for one component within a traditional degree program, such as for out-of-class learning or independent study; or (3) contracting for a complete educational experience or program.

Basically, contracting for grades in particular courses involves an agreement between the teacher and the student at the begin-

---

*For more on this relationship, see Mayville, 1973, p. 1.

ning of the course as to the grade the student expects to receive and the amount and quality of work he is expected to produce to earn this grade. Edward Dash states the rationale for this form of contracting in these words:

> One way to reduce the problem of ambiguous teacher expectations of pupil behavior is to make instructional objectives crystal clear. Some educators have found that the contract system of teaching facilitates not only the clear understanding of objectives, but also increases the active participation of students in the learning process . . . . the contract helps to make learning more realistic by focusing student attention on the process by which he becomes an active learner" (1970, p. 23).

The advantages of this approach include the fact that students are aware of what is expected of them right from the start of the course and that, because the contract is not necessarily limited in time, they may progress at their own rate without the fear and anxiety associated with falling behind. Frequently, as well, this kind of contract specifies various plateaus of performance for which students can earn higher grades with more and better quality work than they have contracted to produce.

Learning contracts, in contrast—the subject of this book—may not necessarily involve prior agreement over an eventual grade but instead agreement over almost everything else about a learning experience: its focus, scope, methods, duration, and evaluation. The difference between contract learning as one component within a traditional college or university program and that which constitutes the student's complete educational experience is best illustrated by the differences between Justin Morrill College on the one hand and the other institutions depicted in earlier chapters. As John Duley's description of Justin Morrill indicates, students there have three contract learning options—out-of-class, including field study, independent study, and field education—as a part of their total program. In contrast, New College at Sarasota allows its students to contract for their entire curriculum by completing nine ten-week contracts, four of which may be earned off campus. Students at Empire State College submit a "Degree Program," including information about their competence, knowledge, and personal development gained prior to enrollment, for approval by a faculty committee, after which this statement becomes the general framework within which the student pursues individual contracts designed in collaboration with his faculty mentor who plays a much larger role in guiding the student's entire studies than does the typical faculty member in a conventional departmentalized institution.

Students in the University Without Walls unit at Morgan State University begin their program by documenting their prior learning experiences, then negotiate additional educational experiences based on their own goals, and complete their work for the degree by a series of completed learning contracts that are reviewed during three evaluation sessions. Students at the New College of the University of Alabama are expected to develop their long range educational and vocational goals and then utilize learning contracts on a semester by semester basis to achieve those goals appropriate for their undergraduate program, whether through regular on-campus classes, independent study, out-of-class learning, special interdisciplinary seminars, or credit for prior learning.

Despite the diversity of approaches within these two current major types of learning contract plans, several basic elements common to all present approaches should be considered in any future approaches to contract learning.

First, contract learning requires a clear statement of learning objectives. This fact has implications both for students and for faculty mentors, since such goal setting is not typically a part of the training of either group. Contract learning requires not only a willingness on the part of faculty to ask students, "What are your educational and vocational goals?" but also an ability to assist students with the development of objectives that can be translated into meaningful learning activities appropriate both for the student, the faculty member, and the institution which is certifying the educational quality of the activities.

Second, learning contracts should not be seen as immutable. Educational contracts in any setting should have the capacity of being changed and should be seen as statements which may be modified for appropriate shifts in educational or vocational goals. While total lack of structure and complete fluidity is not desirable, the quality of flexibility based on considered change in a student's plans and goals should be the hallmark of viable learning contract programs.

Third, the student and mentor should agree on a statement of methodology, approach, and evaluation before any contract is implemented. This statement should describe in as much detail as possible the way the contract will be fulfilled, including appropriate readings, writing, or other creative and work activities, the amount of time to be spent in these endeavors, and the techniques of assessment to be employed in their evaluation. Indeed, this mutually negotiated and agreed-upon statement is the defining characteristic of contract learning plans, distinguishing them from more common forms of individualized education such as tutorials and independent study.

Fourth, contract learning should be characterized by due process. Either one responsible individual or a group of individuals with competence to supervise and evaluate the experience should participate in the experience from the beginning. The possibility of outside examiners, a review committee composed of persons not directly involved in the contract program, and an appeal body should be present in the event that disagreement arises between student and mentor over fulfillment of the terms of the contract. While the existence of a review committee may create additional problems of articulation and interpretation for the contract learning program, it can allay the anxiety of many faculty members regarding contracts in institutions that are particularly traditional in nature.

Fifth, systematic evaluation should be characteristic of any contract learning program. As Hodgkinson pointed out above in Chapter Three, a mid-course correction may occasionally be necessary in the evaluation approach taken, but periodic and final evaluations are essential to determine the credits to be granted for the learning experience. Some institutions, such as the University Without Walls unit at Morgan State University, specify written evaluations by both the student and the faculty mentor. Others may employ oral examinations or multiple assessments of the product of the experience—whether a formal paper, a work of art, a photographic essay, a computer program, an oral presentation, or any other evidence. In all cases, evaluation is not only one of the most vital components of the learning contract approach in terms of successful experiences and growth for the student, it is one of the most essential in terms of the credibility of the program and the creditability of student learning for those who must review the program for approval and support and others, such as employers or graduate school admissions committees, who review students' experiences for credentialing or certification.

Finally and most important, a successful contract learning program requires a new role for faculty members—one different from either that of lecturer or instructor, conveying information to students, or that of faculty advisor, merely approving student course choices and telling the student what he can and cannot take. This new role has been symbolized by such new phrases as *mentor* and *learning facilitator*: it is that of diagnostician, assisting the student with the development and clarification of learning goals, self-understanding, and self-direction. This role stems from the principle that we teach not necessarily by precept but by example in situations, as in contract learning programs, where the interaction between the student and faculty member is great. Among the qualifications for a mentor are these specified by Hartwick College in New York State for its faculty: (1) Know the course requirements. (2) Know the student's college goals. (3) Know the student's career goals. (4) Help the student design ways to apply his goals. (5) Share a common interest, a class or major. (6) Be familiar with offerings in other fields. And (7) Be well aware of college resources (Maxwell, 1972, p. 1). In addition, if the contract program aims not merely at learning subject matter in specialized areas but also at the total development of the student as a person —socially, emotionally, physically as well as intellectually—the role of the mentor as a diagnostician for more than just the cognitive development of each student must include awareness of these other growth needs of the student as well.

For institutions considering one or another approach to contract learning, it may be well to itemize the advantages or strengths of present programs which manifest the above characteristics and then list the disadvantages or weaknesses of learning contracts.

In *Education and Identity,* Chickering identified several educational conditions of colleges which can positively or negatively influence student development, such as the development of identity, the development of purpose, and the development of a sense of competence in interpersonal relationships. His evidence suggests that such growth is not fostered "when few electives are offered, when books and print are the sole object of study, when teaching is by lecture, when evaluation is frequent and competitive" (1971, p. 148). Instead, these qualities are developed when students are offered choice, diversity, interaction, and responsibility. As with other forms of individualized programs, learning contracts offer these conditions to students. In traditional learning settings, structures are established which it is felt will produce the learning situation desired. These structures are designed to focus and constrain the learning experience. With individualized approaches such as learning contracts, rather than making these structures or constraints the emphasis at the outset, an effort is made to respond to the fact of individual differences and to tailor-make a learning situation by adding structure only as it *supports* learning.

In contrast to more traditional forms of individualized study, contract learning reduces ambiguity on the part of the student in the learning process because it requires specificity as to learning goals, methodology, and evaluation techniques at the outset of the contract, as the earlier chapters in this book by Feeney and Riley and by Chickering indicate. Moreover, the work involved in the student's development of the contract and in negotiating its provisions with the mentor can be a significant learning experience in and of itself.

It can also be demonstrated that the role of faculty and staff members is modified in such a way that they are no longer the source of all truth and wisdom or the authority in the learning process when contracts are used successfully. *Some* of the other strengths of the contract learning process include the fact that it demands student initiative since it individualizes the learning experience in a way that should make it more relevant to the student's interests and needs. It is then possible to capitalize on student motivation to learn and permits a kind of freedom with responsibility which is a vital part of the educational process for students at any age. The successful implementation of contract learning programs also requires student and faculty dialogue which unfortunately is not something that takes place with great regularity in many higher education settings. The importance of students being involved in determining the kind of feedback and evaluation approach in the learning process is also something which should not be minimized. The fact, as Bilorusky points out, that contract learning may also accommodate institutional and professional demands since it permits the certification of students and satisfies an accountability need on the part of institutions and society is also an advantage which should be listed on the positive side of the ledger. Finally, the fact that the contract model prepares people to live in a "future oriented" society should be seen as a major advantage. It is obvious that the importance of choice and the availability of many alternatives and options makes the need greater for persons in the educational process to develop an ability to deal with principles and concepts, to make educated choices, and to be much more involved in the teaching and learning process. Contract learning certainly encourages this kind of active involvement.

There are, however, a number of weaknesses or disadvantages which need to be considered if a complete picture of contract learning is to be provided. It may well be that for a number of students there is a kind of undue pressure placed on the student which heightens the anxiety level during the learning process. In a purist sense, there could be a kind of insecurity created which encourages the student to seek relief through performance in a competitive manner which may take away from the questioning, experimenting and probing approach requisite for significant learning to occur. In addition, as pointed out by Bilorusky and Butler, there is a kind of covert relationship many times between the student and faculty member or mentor in the contract learning process. In some cases, students are given the responsibility but little power or authority in determining the bounds of the learning experience or its certification to the satisfaction of the faculty member or mentor. In these cases, there may be a misguided attempt to produce independence through paternalism—a dilemma that many of us have faced in child rearing. Feeney and Riley also point out that contract learning has not brought the educational "drama" that some had predicted. If as pointed out by these authors contract learning is an open-ended registration form which is given substance by the collection of course offerings and other resources made available by the college, contract learning may not impose any new models or develop problem solving skills. This is exacerbated by the fact that most college faculties are composed of persons who come out of traditional graduate training programs so that it is possible for the disciplinary values and faculty priorities from these kinds of background situations to be utilized in such a way that the educational contract promotes a highly conservative and structured learning situation. Duley also cautions that, due to the time commitments necessary to adequately develop a contract learning experience, many faculty members may not require as much specificity as they should particularly with independent study options.

A number of the authors point out very clearly that contract learning demands more of the student in the way of motivation. It is obvious that some students are more inclined than others to take advantage of this kind of added involvement in the learning process. Duley itemized an experience with the Field Education Program in Public Affairs and the Arts that went too far in placing responsibility on the students to do the initial identification of issues and to develop original proposals. It is also obvious that while contracts allow for increased creativity, they do not insure or create creativity. In an era of varied marketing approaches to entice students into higher education, it should also be noted that this particular innovative approach does not necessarily enhance the "marketability" of the institution as witnessed by the situation of financial exigency at New College-Sarasota. It seems evident that contract learning programs require a broader range of faculty competence, not necessarily in terms of the knowledge areas but in terms of the ability to work well with students as an advisor, mentor as well as supervisor of the learning experience. One final possible negative point should be noted for consideration. The taproot concept that learning needs to be linked to the individual student's interests and aspirations rather than enforcement by the college of a standardized learning experience for all persons attending is a basic ingredient of contract learning efforts. Various program dimensions then become the vehicles for assuring institutional responsiveness that permits the kind of flexibility necessary to achieve these goals. And yet it appears that this ideal—the realization of individual potential through contract learning—becomes clouded and polemical as liberal arts education is mixed with various approaches to general education and vocational preparation is added as another variable. The need for a more effective integration of the goals of the liberal arts versus vocational preparation in the context of contract learning raises serious questions about where the liberalizing educational experience stops and training begins. If taken seriously, the goal of individualization through contract learning throws the college degree "up for grabs" in terms of experience needed, time taken, and such issues as "How do I know when I am through?" The learning contract as the vehicle for individualization seems to be one strategy for flexibility that permits and requires on a regular basis the questioning of how each individual student is to pursue his or her educational and vocational goals but does not lessen this dilemma.

A number of additional factors need to be considered. In an era of already limited financial resources the issue of financing contract learning programs becomes even more critical. Although the cost of developing a contract learning system may be minimal, as pointed out by Feeney and Riley, the long range expense of an individualized curricular approach may be much more than the traditional type, particularly as one contemplates the need for additional training of faculty and staff in the area of advising and facilitating the learning experience. It was pointed out that, with institutions having a contract learning program located within a larger institutional setting, it is possible to run the contract learning program inexpensively such as that illustrated by the University Without Walls unit at Morgan State. Another point here is illustrated by New College at the University of Alabama in that this contract learning program has been able to generate additional resources from private foundations and federal government sources so that these monies could be utilized across a large university to promote non-traditional approaches to teaching and learning and go beyond just the contract learning program of the New College. The question certainly remains as to how this kind of individualization approach can be maximized and yet retain the economies of scale of institutions. While a system of private tutorials or a "de-schooled society" is not being advocated by any of the authors, either for educational or financial reasons, the need to make this kind of individualization economically viable becomes even more critical for the future. As Craig and others point out, however, even though learning contracts may take extra time and may not be totally cost efficient, in an era of dwindling enrollments institutions may be in a better position to respond to the needs of the individual through contract learning programs as they will be able to take the time to work more with individual students rather than to gear up for the next major increase in enrollment or a new building program. The number of examples cited illustrate the value of this kind of approach for some students in spite of some of the apparent unanswered questions.

Similarly, additional research data is needed to indicate more clearly what happens to students who go through these kinds of contract learning programs. Chickering presents survey data indicating student satisfaction with the contract learning process and yet additional information is needed as to the effectiveness of this approach as it meets stated objectives versus the utilization of other approaches in the teaching and learning process. It needs to also be mentioned that the time frame within which most contract learning programs have been operating is so limited that it may be expected that such research activity would yield limited results although Craig and others did include such information. The New College at the University of Alabama found that a student's chances for futher study or employment were not jeopardized by participation in this kind of individualized program. This was based on not only work at the New College but also on a series of visits under a Title III Grant a few years ago to a number of innovative colleges in the United Staes. In fact, by careful attention to certain basic professional and graduate requirements which can be achieved through regular courses or through experiential learning equivalents, the contract format may provide a student with a vehicle for obtaining a type of preparation which will be more appealing to external agencies. Since the student frequently has an opportunity through depth-study programs to preserve basic courses as far as specified course requirements for graduate study or to substitute equivalent experiences, they may be protected in terms of their future area of specialization at the graduate level. It does appear, however, that explanation as to what occurred in some of the different kinds of learning experiences that are possible in contract learning programs is necessary for graduate, professional or employer understanding of what happened.

Preliminary research at the University of Alabama and elsewhere seems to indicate that larger businesses and industries usually are going to provide their new employees with necessary specialized training soon after hiring so that coming from a more individualized program is not a major difficulty. In fact, there is a preference expressed many times by these external agencies for the student who has had to play a much greater role in shaping his undergraduate program. It would appear that smaller businesses and industries, firms of up to ten professional employees, prefer the individual to come through a fairly traditional program. The most difficulty seems to be in meeting certain rigid certification requirements for some national professional societies. The student is often forced to make a decision as to whether he would like to be certified by such a professional organization or would prefer more flexibility in his program although there are a number of instances where even these requirements have been translated into acceptable educational experiences that are other than the traditional. Similarly, there are indications that state certification agencies for teaching can be flexible in accepting different educational experiences for equivalent requirements for certification. This usually, however, requires extra effort with the on-campus Department of Education so that the learning experiences accomplished through the contract program can be translated into understandable and acceptable equivalencies or recognized as being different approaches to learning of value in their own right. It should also be noted that regional accrediting associations are in the process of developing their own procedures which encourage the consideration of accreditation of innovative programs based upon different standards than those utilized for the evaluation of traditional programs. The experience of the Union for Experimenting Colleges and Universities of being granted Correspondence Status from the North Central Accrediting Association and the experience of the New College at the University of Alabama with the Southern Association of Colleges and Schools is encouraging along these lines. While some individuals stress the need to completely disregard concern for accreditation, change which will have meaning beyond a particular local setting has already been supported by regional accrediting bodies and it would seem that the greatest opportunities to maximize the impact of non-traditional approaches of value would be to continue to work with accrediting associations to do better the job of self-study of both traditional and non-traditional programs.

In addition, the need for a planned program of evaluation of the use of learning contracts in any setting seems imperative. At a time when the accountability issues loom larger in society, it no longer suffices to say that "intuitively we think that what we are doing here is right." On the one hand, supporters of management systems who are primarily concerned with quantitative criteria and cost-effectiveness must be dealt with. Certainly assessment must be made in terms of dollars spent but also in other terms. The importance of gathering qualitative data cannot be stressed too much if there is to be any effective evaluation of the learning contract program. There is an obvious need for intensive longitudinal follow-up studies of students coming out of these programs. (See Hodkinson, 1974, p. 82.)

More attention must also be given to the fact that contract learning redefines faculty roles, which necessitates special training opportunities for faculty and staff members. There is some indication that faculty members who express an interest in working in these kinds of programs are more committed to effective undergraduate teaching and advising than they are to placing the top priority on research and publication. This means a number of things including the development of a reward system that encourages recognition for the successful performance of the role of mentor, advisor, or a facilitative role for faculty members versus the more traditional emphasis on research and publication. Faculty and staff development in learning contract programs becomes even more critical in the area of changing values and feelings about what is effective teaching and learning. The problem of re-tooling existing faculty and staff to be able to teach differently with the new styles in a contract learning program leads one to conclude that the goal is to assist faculty with learning how to supervise learning rather than to dispense it. Shifting the center from teaching per se to student-centered learning so that the faculty member is viewed as a co-learner seems important. Developing some form of recognized agency within the faculty to deal with new teaching approaches, the use of faculty workshops and institutes, released time for faculty development activities, faculty and staff growth contracts, faculty peer group evaluation as well as evaluation by adminstrators and students, use of video tape and other audiovisual equipment so that the faculty member may see himself in action—are all ideas to be considered. In addition, assisting the faculty member with understanding resources outside of their own specific area of competence represents another training need for individuals working with contract learning programs. As Chickering points out, these resources may range widely but should be representative of intellectually sound learning processes designed by persons into whose specific areas of competence they fall. This may mean learning processes that occur in the context of tutorial relationships, courses at the parent or at other institutions, field experiences, correspondence study, or other learning experiences developed to meet the objectives of a particular student's program. Similarly, there are special orientation needs for students to be able to better understand the many dimensions of contract learning programs as they make the transition from traditional learning situations to that of non-traditional learning environments.

Certainly there are other aspects of contract learning which have implications for the educational process. For example, the approach to shared governance which characterizes many of the institutions that are utilizing contract learning programs is an additional issue for contemplation. When students are more involved in shaping their educational experiences through the utilization of contracts, this usually means there is an interest in greater involvement and more active representation on governing bodies of various campus decision making units. Frequently, this means greater representation not only for students but also a shared approach on behalf of faculty, administrators, maintenance staff, secretaries, alumni and other representatives of constituent groups.

The evidence is certainly not all in regarding the effectiveness of individualization approaches, and more particularly the use of the contract learning model. Many institutions are implementing contract learning programs with the hope that they will be part of an academic reform movement in higher education which will enhance the opportunities for each student to find a set of learning experiences which will best help him to create for himself a fuller and more satisfying life. The history of American higher education is replete with examples of various approaches to individualization of the undergraduate experience. President Eliot's elective system at Harvard, permitting students to select courses within broad distribution requirements, alternative paths to meet specific competency requirements, multiple tracking and ability grouping, student-designed majors and student-designed courses, directed readings, independent study, and tutorials are some of the approaches taken which contrast with the Lancastrian system of mass producing students through a totally prescribed and regimented sequential curriculum.

It should be clearly stated that the author is not advocating contract learning as a panacea for higher education nor an all out "student right or wrong" movement. Certainly more needs to be done to determine appropriate limits for what represents viable learning experiences within the various approaches to contract learning. But we do know that students entering college today differ widely in the abilities, their high school experiences, their goals, their demographic characteristics and that the demand will become greater for a wider spectrum of educational activity from which students at all levels may choose. As noted at the outset of this book, the recommendations emerging from the various Commission reports which have appeared in the last decade all argue for more variety in college programs, for more alternatives in curricula and for a greater emphasis in meeting the needs of the individual student rather than for pre-packaging educational experiences with the assumption that these experiences are right for all. The use of the contract learning approach offers a viable option to achieve these goals.

BIBLIOGRAPHY

BALDWIN, R. E., "Down with the Degree Structure." *Change,* Volume 5, Number 2, March 1973. 50–55.

BENNIS, W., and SLATER, P. *The Temporary Society.* New York: Harper and Row, 1968.

BERTE, N. R., and UPSHAW, C. "Student Life Studies: An Action Research Option," *National Association of Student Personnel Administrators Journal,* July 1971, 9 (1), 77–80.

BILORUSKY, J. *Reconstitution at Berkeley: The Quest for Collective Self-determination.* Unpublished doctoral dissertation. University of California, Berkeley, 1972.

BLOOM, B. S. (Ed.) *Taxonomy of Educational Objectives Handbook I: Cognitive Domain.* New York: David McKay, 1956.

BLUMER, H. *Symbolic Interactionism: Perspective and Method.* Englewood Cliffs, N. J.: Prentice-Hall, 1969.

BROWN, W. F. *Student to Student Counseling: An Approach to Motivating Academic Achievement.* San Marcos, Texas: Hogg Foundation Research Series, 1965.

BUTLER, H., and BILORUSKY, J. *Open Curricula: Experimenting Communities for Professionals.* Paper presented at the annual program meeting of the Council on Social Work Education. San Francisco, Feb. 1973.

CARNAP, R. *Philosophical Foundation of Physics.* New York: Basic Books, 1966.

CARNEGIE COMMISSION ON HIGHER EDUCATION, *Less Time, More Options: Education Beyond the High School.* New York: McGraw-Hill, 1971.

CARNEGIE COMMISSON ON HIGHER EDUCATION. *Reform on Campus.* New York: McGraw-Hill, 1972.

CHICKERING, A. W. *Education and Identity.* San Francisco: Jossey-Bass, 1971.

COMMISSION ON NON-TRADITIONAL STUDY. In *The Chronicle of Higher Education,* Feb. 5, 1973.

DASH, E. "Contract for Grades." ERIC Clearinghouse on Higher Education, 1970, p. 231.

DEWEY, J. *Experience and Education.* New York: Macmillan, 1938.

DIXON, J. P. "Personalized Higher Education: Ideas and Issues." in W. J. Mintor (Ed.), *The Individual and the System.* Boulder: Western Interstate Commission for Higher Education, 1967.

DRESSEL, P. L. (Ed.) *The New Colleges: Toward an Appraisal.* Iowa City, Iowa: American College Testing Program, 1971.

ELMENDORF, J. "New College-Sarasota, Florida." In P. L. Dressel (Ed.), *The New Colleges: Toward an Appraisal.* Iowa City, Iowa: American College Testing Program, 1971.

EMPIRE STATE COLLEGE. *Catalog.* Saratoga Springs, N. Y., 1973.

ERISCON, S. C. "The Teacher, the Book and the Student's Private Knowledge." In J. W. Mintor (Ed.), *The Individual and the System.* Boulder: Western Interstate Commission for Higher Education, 1967.

FEENEY, J. "Some Notes on the Learning Contract System in an Undergraduate College." Sarasota, Fla.: New College, 1973.

GLASER, B., and STRAUSS, A. *The Discovery of Grounded Theory.* Chicago: Aldine, 1967.

GOULD, S. B. (Ed.) *Diversity by Design.* San Francisco: Jossey-Bass. 1973.

HODGKINSON, H. L. "Assessment and Reward Systems." In G. K. Smith (Ed.), *New Teaching, New Learning.* Washington D. C.: American Association for Higher Education, 1971a.

HODGKINSON, H. L. *Institutions in Transition: A Study of Change in Higher Education.* New York: McGraw-Hill, 1971b.

HODGKINSON, H. L. *A Manual for the Evaluation of Innovative Programs and Practices in Higher Education.* Berkeley, Cal.: Center for Research and Development in Higher Education, 1974.

HOOK, S. "John Dewey and His Betrayers." *Change,* Nov. 1971, 7, 22–26.

HUNT, D. E. "Matching Models and Moral Training." In C. M. Beck, B. S. Crittenden, and E. V. Sullivan (Eds.), *Moral Education.* Toronto: University of Toronto Press, 1971.

ILLICH, I. "After Deschooling What?" *Social Policy,* Vol. 2, No. 3, Sept./Oct. 1971, 5–13.

JENCKS, C., and RIESMAN, D. *The Academic Revolution.* Garden City, N. Y.: Doubleday, 1968.

KITTRIE, N. *The Right to be Different.* Baltimore: Johns Hopkins Press, 1971.

KOHLBERG, L. "Stages of Moral Development as a Basis for Moral Education." In C. M. Beck, B. S. Crittenden, and E. V. Sullivan (Eds.), *Moral Education.* Toronto: University of Toronto Press, 1971.

LOEVINGER, J. "The Meaning and Measurement of Ego Development." *American Psychologist,* 1966, *21,* 195–206.

LOEVINGER, J., and WESSLER, R. *Measuring Ego Development.* (Vol. I) San Francisco: Jossey-Bass, 1970.

LOVELL, B. "An Open Mind and Simple Equipment." *The Times (London) Educational Supplement,* Dec. 22, 1972.

MAGER, R. F. Developing Attitude Toward Learning. Belmont, Calif.: Fearon Publishers, 1962.

MAXWELL, H. B. *Evidences of Change in the Individual Student.* Proposal to Committee for Institutional Research. Hartwick College, Dec. 1972.

MAYHEW, L. B. *The Literature of Higher Education 1971.* San Francisco: Jossey-Bass, 1971.

MAYVILLE, W. "Contract Learning." *Research Currents,* ERIC Clearinghouse on Higher Education, Dec. 1973, p. 1.

NOONAN, J. "Curricular Change: A Strategy for Improving Teaching." In G. K. Smith (Ed.), *The Expanded Campus.* San Francisco: Jossey-Bass, 1972.

OTTAWA UNIVERSITY SELF STUDY COMMITTEE. *The New Plan of Education for Ottawa University.* (2nd ed.) Ottawa, Kansas: Ottawa University, 1970.

PEARL, A. "The More We Change, the Worse We Get." *Change,* Mar./Apr. 1970, pp. 39–44.

PLATO. "The Republic." In R. M. Hutchins (Ed.), *Great Books of the Western World.* (Vol. VII) London: Encyclopaedia Britannica, 1952.

SANFORD, N. *Where Colleges Fail.* San Francisco: Jossey-Bass, 1967.

SNYDER, B. *The Hidden Curriculum*. New York: Alfred Knopf, 1971.

THOMAS, E. J. "Selecting Knowledge for Behavioral Science." In *Building Social Work Knowledge*: *Report of a Conference.* New York: National Association of Social Workers, 1967.

TOFFLER, A. *Future Shock*. New York: Bantam Books, 1970.

UNIVERSITY WITHOUT WALLS. Summary Statement. July 1971. Union for Experimenting Colleges and Universities, Yellow Springs, Ohio.

VICKERS, D. F. "The Learning Consultant: A Response to the External Degree Learner." *The Journal of Higher Education,* June 1973, *44.*

WATERMAN, A. "Learning by Contract." *Change,* Winter 1972–1973, *8,* 12ff.

YOUNG, D. P., and GERING, D. D. *The College Student and the Course.* Asheville, N. C.: College Administration Publications, 1973.

INDEX

ADMINISTRATION OF
CONTRACT LEARNING
  Admission to programs, 77-80, 104-105
  Options offered, 80-82
  Aims of contract learning, 3-11
  Attrition, 53, 56-58
  Certification problem, 160-166
  Costs, 60-61, 84-86
  Depth-study program, 108
  Faculty competence, 59-60
    development for, 27-28
  Faculty facilitators, 177
  Faculty mentors, 177
  Faculty roles redefined, 184-185
  Faculty-student interaction, 51-52, 55-56
  Forms for contracts, 37-50
  Goal setting, 13, 83-84
  Impact of contracts on campus, 28-29
  Interdisciplinary seminars, 106-108
  Learning consultants, 14

  advising the students, 13-19
  refining the goals, 19-20
  Need for differentiated staffing, 29-30
  New College, Universities Without Walls, etc.
    as experimental bases, 120-121
  Program design, 43, 51
  Subject areas most amenable to contracts, 51
  Specimens of contracts, 44-51
  Teaching techniques for contract learning, 51, 54-56
  Types of contracts, 43

EVALUATION OF
CONTRACT LEARNING
  Acceptability of, 182-184
  Advantages of, 177-179
  Assessment of, 73-76
    as to administration, 119-120
    as to faculty, 117-118

as to students, 111-116,
   118-119
by consultants, 117
by students, 176-177
by unobtrusive measures,
   116-117
Costs of, 60-61
Effectiveness of, 186
   case studies, 97-101
Instruments for, 25-27
Self-evaluation, 21-24
Strategies for, 24-25
Student response, 86-96
Weaknesses of, 59, 179-182
   solipsism encouraged by,
   61
(*See also* Goals of Contract
   Learning, Individualized
   Learning.)

FACTORS PREDISPOSING
TO LEARNING BY
CONTRACT
Atrophy of respect for traditional curriculum, 34-36,
   58
Loss of institutional power,
   33
Shift of authority from institution to individual, 36
Open admissions entailing
   greater diversity of students, 77-82
Increasing complexity of
   technological and cultural
   needs, 122-123

GOALS OF CONTRACT
LEARNING
Intellectual competence,
   knowledge, 63-65
Intellectual skills, 63-72
   Comprehension, 65-67
   Application, 67-68
   Analysis, 68-70
   Synthesis, 70-71
   Evaluation, 71-72
Case studies of contract ef-
   fectiveness, 97-101
Individualization of learning
   through contracts, 13, 80-
   82, 147-151 (*See also* In-
   dividualized Learning.)

INDIVIDUALIZED
LEARNING
"Closed" contracts, 148-149
"Open" contracts, 149-151
   Field study contracts, 124-
   133
   Independent study con-
   tracts, 134-137
   Field education contracts,
   137-142
Improvisational Learning
   Script improvisation, 152
   Continuous self-confronta-
   tion, 152-153
   Developmental themes,
   154-156
   Community experiences,
   157-160, 169-172
   Collaborative advising, 166

DATE DUE

DE 05 '83	DEC 13 '83		
GAYLORD			PRINTED IN U.S.A